SHADOW

CHRISTIANS

SHADOW CHRISTIANS

MAKING

AN IMPACT

WHEN NO ONE

KNOWS

YOUR NAME

JEFF IORG

B&H
PUBLISHING
NASHVILLE, TENNESSEE

Published by B&H Publishing Group
Nashville, Tennessee

Dewey Decimal Classification: 259
Subject Heading: CHRISTIAN LIFE / MINISTRY /
CHURCH WORK

Cover design by Spencer Fuller, FaceOut.

1 2 3 4 5 6 • 24 23 22 21 20

With Appreciation For

Eric Espinoza,

the shadow Christian
who worked tirelessly and persistently
to make this book a reality.

CONTENTS

Chapter 1: Life in the Shadows 1
You matter, even if you are not well-known.

Part One: God Chooses Shadow Christians

Chapter 2: God Knows Us Intimately 15
Through Jesus, shadow Christians know God intimately.

Chapter 3: God Loves Us Tenderly 33
Through Jesus, shadow Christians experience God's tender love.

Chapter 4: God Values Us Highly 51
Shadow Christians are valued by God.

Part Two: God Uses Shadow Christians

Chapter 5: We Experience God's Power 71
Shadow Christians experience God's power.

Chapter 6: We Share the Gospel. 93
Shadow Christians share the gospel.

Chapter 7: We Are the Ministry Workforce 115
Shadow Christians are the ministry workforce.

Chapter 8: We Do the Dirty Work 133
Shadow Christians do the dirty work.

Chapter 9: We Lead Churches 149
Shadow Christians lead churches.

Chapter 10: We Start Churches and Ministries 167
Shadow Christians start new churches and ministries.

Chapter 11: We Fund Churches and Ministries. 185
Shadow Christians fund ministry.

Conclusion

Chapter 12: Staying in the Shadows 203
You matter, but making your name well-known doesn't.

Notes 209

CHAPTER 1

LIFE IN THE SHADOWS

Names matter.

Expectant parents spend hours poring over baby name books, trying to find just the right name for a child on the way. Many cultures attach meaning to a child's name, hoping the name will motivate the child to develop certain character qualities or live up to family expectations. Some people have family names they pass on to their children, creating "Juniors" and "Treys," perpetuating family lineage and tradition. Teenage girls still scrawl their first name with their boyfriend's last name, trying a new identity on for size and fantasizing what married life might be like. And some women prefer keeping their own name or hyphenating both names. Either choice underscores the point—names matter.

Our culture values big names. We encourage people to make a name for themselves or get their name up in lights. When we are planning a major event, we try to get a celebrity on the program—a big-name entertainer, athlete, politician, or other well-known figure to boost attendance. Some people are so well-known they go by only one name—Bach and Mozart, Madonna and Bono, Tiger and Serena. Groupies even take on the name of their icons—Taylor has her Swifties and the Grateful Dead their Dead Heads.

Most of us want our name spelled and pronounced correctly. This has been a challenge for me over the years, since Iorg is not a common name. The uniqueness of my name makes it special to me, even though it's almost always mispronounced and variant spellings make checking into hotels an adventure. Over the years, I have been Mr. Lorg or Mr. Torg or Mr. Long or Mr. Tong about as often as Mr. Iorg. Just to set the record straight, my last name is I-O-R-G. It's pronounced like *forge* without the letter *f*.

Our name originated in 1857 at Ellis Island, New York. The oldest instance of our name in print is on the manifest for a ship called the *Bazaar* (not the *Bizarre*, which given some of our family history might have been more appropriate). The European heritage and spelling of our name has been lost. Our family genealogists, along with professionals in the field, have turned over every imaginable rock trying to unearth the history of our name—to no avail. When Iorg was entered into the ship's logbook, the Iorg family name was born. Whoever he was and wherever he came from, he established a new identity and family tree. And we have been dealing with the name consequences ever since.

Names matter because they communicate identity. They are how we differentiate people. They are a part of what makes a person unique. Underscoring this, some people come up with unusual names or unusual spellings of common names to create distinction. Christy becomes Christi, Kristi, Krysti, or Chrysty. We use the concept of naming to give a compliment (she made a name for herself) and point out shortcomings (he's a friend in name only). Names communicate who we are, positively and negatively.

Names are how we record history and mark historical eras. Global history revolves around names like Augustine, Attila, and Mandela. Religious figures like Jesus and Mohammed mark movements, while other leaders lend their name to religions like Buddhism. In American history, Washington, Jefferson, and Adams are towering names among the founding fathers. Lincoln and the Roosevelts are named on any list of greatest American presidents. Reagan and Obama are iconic names in recent history, representing modern golden eras for their respective political parties. Negative examples also become names to avoid—no one names their child Hitler, Judas, or Nero.

Names are also consequential in biblical history. Abraham, Moses, Joshua, David, Isaiah, and Elijah are major characters in the Old Testament. Dozens of characters are named in the New Testament as well. Some are major players—like Peter, Paul, Matthew, Mark, Luke, and John (named in many stories and named as authors of the bulk of the New Testament). There are also countless minor characters—from Alexander to Zacchaeus. By one count, 170 people are named in the New Testament. Clearly, many biblical characters were well-known enough to be named—for one reason or another—in the biblical record. Following their example, celebrating their accomplishments, and learning from their mistakes are important ways to grow spiritually.

In all these ways and more, names matter.

Until they don't.

Why the Omissions?

A few years ago, the story of some anonymous New Testament-era preachers caught my attention. Their riveting story became an important part of my story (more about that in chapter 10). Broader than what they accomplished, however, studying them led to several compelling questions: *Why are some biblical characters named and others not named? Why did Jesus call some people by name and leave others in anonymity? Why are some people singled out, by name, for relatively inconsequential contributions, while others, not named, did things that changed the world? Why do some people get their name in the paper while others are left out?*

Back when dinosaurs roamed the earth, something called a newspaper was tossed on your front porch every morning. Publishers used ink and paper to produce the best news source available. That's how information was stored and shared before the digital revolution put this book on your phone or e-reader.

Particularly in small-town papers that focused on local news, getting your name in the paper was a big deal. From football stars to science-fair winners, debutantes to socialites, and even people being promoted at work— getting your name in the paper was an honor. It meant community recognition, personal achievement, and a permanent record of your success. My youth baseball experiences, particularly one glorious summer of winning a series of all-star tournaments, were chronicled by our local newspaper. Those clippings are still in a scrapbook in my garage almost fifty years later. Getting my name in the paper was a big deal.

In a far more significant way, some names are recorded in the Bible. Those names are printed on vastly more important paper. Their stories chronicle the contributions specific individuals made to the progress of God's kingdom. Their names are associated with miraculous exploits and colossal failures. They are superstars and villains whose actions have been memorialized for centuries. Since the Bible is an inspired book, inclusion of these names is significant. Following the same reasoning, the omission of names from important stories must also be significant. That leads to the seminal question that motivated me to write this book:

Why were some biblical characters unnamed, and what can we learn from their stories?

And growing out of that question, even more importantly:

How can Christians who serve in the shadows today make a significant impact?

Significance in the Shadows

Shadow Christians are people who work in dimly lit margins, in the shadows created by the spotlight shining on others. They are believers who serve quietly, often anonymously, doing the work that keeps churches, organizations, families, and communities functioning. Shadow Christians make an impact even when no one knows their names. They care for children, sponsor student events, drive elderly friends to medical appointments, prepare meals others enjoy, give money to sustain ministries, set up for meetings, and change diapers (for the very young and the very old). They take on service roles, often several levels down the organizational chart, that help churches and ministries accomplish their mission. Their service makes more visible leaders successful.

Shadow Christians are the unseen army—millions strong—who take their faith seriously, see themselves as role players in God's grand plan, and seldom give any thought to being recognized for their service.

My study of characters in the biblical shadows, unnamed but incredibly significant, led me to two important conclusions:

God chooses and uses shadow Christians.

He relates to them intimately and tenderly, places high value on their anonymous contributions, and

> **Shadow Christians are people who work in dimly lit margins, in the shadows created by the spotlight shining on others.**

uses them as his essential workforce to accomplish amazing things. The answers to the questions above, along with these conclusions, leads to another more personal conclusion:

You matter.

Celebrating Your Role

You are likely a shadow Christian. You don't have thousands of social media followers, have never spoken at a conference, and have never been asked to share your opinion on public issues. You serve in anonymity, and because of that, you may feel what you do is insignificant.

1

You wonder whether what you do, even in ministry for God, really matters to him or makes any difference. Those doubts are baseless. You are as vital to your family, church, and community as the unnamed people in the Bible were to God's plans in their era.

You may also suffer from a spiritual inferiority complex. Since you aren't well-known and don't consider yourself particularly talented, you may wonder why (or even if) God wants to have a personal relationship with you. Given the global fascination with celebrities, it's easy to believe popularity equals significance. That's the way the world system functions but not God's kingdom. God relates to people without regard to popular (and often misguided) evaluations of their loveliness, desirability, or talents. God values people by a different set of standards.

If you struggle with these perspectives, keep reading to discover biblical predecessors who made an impact even though their names were left out of the story. Their examples (limited to New Testament characters to keep the book a manageable length) will reveal and reinforce the conclusions already mentioned: God chooses and uses shadow Christians. Those themes form the two parts of this book. In part one, you will discover how God relates to shadow Christians. We will clarify how God relates to you intimately and loves you tenderly before considering theological themes revealing how much God values what happens in the shadows.

In part two, you will discover how God uses shadow Christians to accomplish his work. You will learn how important you are to advancing God's kingdom, even if no one knows your name. Whether you are a shadow Christian or a person with a higher profile supported by a shadow team, you are about to discover this profound reality: God uses

> **God chooses and uses shadow Christians.**

anonymous people to do amazing things for him—outside the spotlight, without fanfare or accolades.

God chooses people like you to fulfill his mission.

Group Discussion

1. Does anyone in your group have an unusual name or an unusual story associated with their name? If so, ask them to tell their story.

2. Has anyone in your group ever had their "name in the paper" or otherwise publicized in a significant way (not counting self-generated social media)? If so, ask them to tell their story.

3. Since the Bible is inspired, what it includes and excludes are both important. Why do you think the accomplishments of some people are included in the Bible, but their names are omitted? Discuss insights with your small group.

4. Do you have a favorite anonymous person in the Bible? What did they do? Why does their story resonate with you? Share your insights and discuss them with your group.

5. How does this book define a shadow Christian? What questions about shadow Christians do you hope this study will answer? List those questions, discuss them with your group, and agree to work together to search for answers.

6. Who is a shadow Christian who has impacted your life in a positive way? What did you learn from them? What

can you learn from their example of serving in the shadows? Share these stories with your group.

7. As you begin this study, what are some issues you need to resolve to enhance your role as a shadow Christian? Share these concerns with your group, and ask God for insight and growth over the next few weeks.

8. As you prepare to read the next chapter, how does knowing Jesus define your identity and give you purpose? Have you lost a sense of wonder in knowing Jesus personally? Are you comfortable using "intimacy" to describe your relationship with God? Why or why not? Discuss your answers with your group.

PART ONE

GOD CHOOSES
SHADOW CHRISTIANS

CHAPTER 2

GOD KNOWS US INTIMATELY

Shadow Christians are *Christians*, meaning they have become followers of Jesus Christ and adopted his identity as their own. His name means more than our names and much more than nationalities, ethnic backgrounds, or any cultural affinity. Believers aren't hyphenated people with spiritual qualifiers further defining their identity. We are simply *Christians*, which establishes our new identity. Embedded in that relationship is a new purpose in life: magnifying Jesus and accomplishing his mission in the world.

The process for becoming a Christian is summarized in straightforward verses like these: "Therefore repent and turn back, so that your sins may be wiped out" (Acts 3:19) and "For you are saved by grace through faith, and this is not from yourselves; it is God's gift—not from works, so that no one can boast" (Eph. 2:8–9). It's likely most people reading this book have made a personal commitment to Jesus and consider themselves Christians. If you have not done this, perhaps today is your day! You can receive salvation by repenting of your sin and placing faith in Jesus. You can express those commitments through a prayer like this or one in your own words: "God, thank you for loving me. I confess my sin has separated me from you. I turn from living my way and ask you to forgive me and save me. I commit to following you, Jesus, my Lord and Savior, from this day forward. Amen."

Becoming a Christian, even though it may have happened many years ago for you, is a profound experience. Some people who aren't yet believers struggle so much with feelings of inadequacy and condemnation, that they don't really believe they can become Christians. They wonder, *How could Jesus love me?* and *Why would Jesus want a relationship with me?* Many people feel overwhelmed when they discover God loves them so much he sent Jesus to die on the cross as a substitute for them. They are astounded, in light of their sinfulness and shortcomings, that they can have a relationship with God— and more than that, an *intimate* relationship with him.

When God was ready to reveal himself fully, he came as a person. He didn't send an angel to tell us more about himself; he became a person. He didn't set up a website or tell an Instagram story. He showed up with skin on. God came in the person of Jesus. He wanted us to know him personally but also intimately.

Jesus came to be among people, not aloof from them. He walked, talked, laughed, and prayed with people. He slept in the homes of friends, visited their sick relatives, went to funerals, and attended dinner parties. Jesus was not a distant deity demanding homage or respect. He was a flesh-and-blood person who lived among his followers.

Despite how unworthy you may feel, here is an astounding reality: through Jesus, God wants more than a token connection with you. He wants an intimate relationship. He wants you so close you can touch him.

In the Bible, the people who worked around Jesus and with Jesus are often named (like Peter, James, and John). But many of the people who related to him most intimately are unnamed. The people with him when he was most vulnerable, who touched him physically, who met his personal needs, and who served him with no desire for anything in return were anonymous followers. You don't have to be rich, famous, or popular to have an intimate relationship with God through Jesus. *Through Jesus, shadow Christians know God intimately.*

Intimate Service

Touching someone is an intimate act. Even a pat on the shoulder means a relationship has moved to a higher level of comfort or familiarity. Meaningful touch soothes crying babies and assures worried parents. Stroking someone's head or hair brings comfort. Holding hands communicates companionship. Couples in love rest easy in each other's embrace and calmly share personal space. Touching equates with intimacy.

As previously noted, the people who worked with Jesus are often named (like Peter, James, and John). They are described as being with him, in the same locale, but more often as coworkers than intimate followers. An anonymous woman, however, models what it means to have intimacy with Jesus.

A religious leader invited Jesus to dinner, so he "entered the Pharisee's house and reclined at the table. And a woman in the town who was a sinner found out that Jesus was reclining at the table in the Pharisee's house. She brought an alabaster jar of perfume and stood behind him at his feet, weeping, and began to wash his feet with her tears. She wiped his feet with her hair, kissing them and anointing them with the perfume" (Luke 7:36–38).

This is a moving, poignant story of devotion to Jesus expressed through meaningful touch, extravagant giving, selfless service, and emotional vulnerability. This anonymous woman touched Jesus' feet, a debasing act in almost every culture. More than just touching them, she watered them with her tears and wiped them with her hair. She did this while dousing his feet with expensive perfume— an extravagant use of a precious commodity—and then kissing them.

It's hard to imagine more intimate gestures than this woman caressing Jesus' feet with her hands, hair, and lips. All of this occurred at a dinner party in front of multiple guests (the Pharisee, Jesus, and Peter are listed, but others were likely present). The public nature of this woman's service was likely humbling and emotionally draining. On top of this, her moral standing in the community was suspect, which made her presence even more awkward (Luke 7:39).

Jesus used the occasion to teach a valuable lesson about forgiveness (Luke 7:40–43) and confront the Pharisee (and perhaps other guests) about their hypocrisy and judgmental attitude. He responded to the woman's service by telling her, "Your sins are forgiven" (Luke 7:48) and assuring her, "Your faith has saved you" (Luke 7:50). The contrast between the puffed-up religious leaders and this humble woman is stark and revealing. While Jesus had little use for religious bullies, he welcomed broken people into intimate relationship with him.

Shadow Christians can be intimate with Jesus. He isn't a distant god—some far-off deity we summon with loud noises, extravagant displays, or religious tricks. Jesus isn't haughty or stuffy. He welcomes us into his presence—people who come humbly, without pretense, but with sincerity. He wants broken people to touch him, caress him, and kiss him. Jesus is a brother you can hug, not an icon you can't touch.

Devotion and Service

The woman at the Pharisee's house wasn't the only woman to minister to Jesus in this way. On another occasion, Jesus was in Bethany having dinner with his disciples (Matt. 26:6–13; Mark 14:3–9). An unnamed woman "approached him with an alabaster jar of very expensive perfume. She poured it on his head as he was reclining at the table" (Matt. 26:7).[1]

Whoever it was, the disciples were indignant at her actions. They asked, "Why this waste?" and suggested, "This might have been sold for a great deal and given to the poor" (Matt. 26:8b–9). Jesus knew what they were thinking and asked, "Why are you bothering this woman? She has done a noble thing for me. You always have the poor with you, but you do not always have me. By pouring this perfume on my body, she has prepared me for burial" (Matt. 26:10–12).

Jesus couched important insights in this rebuke. First, he revealed his early followers struggled to grasp that our priority is ministry *to* Jesus rather than ministry *for* him. This is still a common problem. We want to do ministry for Jesus. He wants us to do this, but not at the expense of first serving him. We must not lose focus on maintaining personal, intimate devotion to Jesus. Second, he confronted their mistaken belief that extravagance directed toward Jesus somehow exhausts our capacity to serve others. Jesus stated a hard reality, "You will always have the poor with you," to restore perspective to the conversation. Jesus' time on Earth was limited. Poverty would remain a persistent problem that would always need to be addressed. Through how he responded in this situation, Jesus teaches the importance of serving him. We do this today by spending time in private devotion or personal worship. This involves spiritual disciplines like reading the Bible, meditating on biblical insights, praying (perhaps with fasting), and singing worship songs to Jesus.

Christians also serve Jesus by serving others. His frank assessment about the poor acknowledged human needs will always demand our attention. Jesus wasn't advocating we callously ignore those needs. He was prioritizing relating to him above doing work for him. On another occasion, Jesus indicated serving others is one way to express devotion to him. He said, "Then the righteous will answer him, 'Lord when did we see you hungry and feed you, or thirsty and give you something to drink? When did we see you a stranger and take you in, or without clothes and clothe you? When did we see you sick, or in prison, and visit you?' And the King will answer them, 'Truly I tell you, whatever you did for one of the least of these brothers and sisters of mine, you did for me'" (Matt. 25:37–40).

Personal devotion to Jesus versus serving others to express devotion to Jesus isn't an either/or proposition. It's a priority problem. We must first serve Jesus through personal devotion, then through practical service to others. When the latter takes precedence, we wear ourselves out with self-motivated attempts to gain his favor. Burnout often results. You may find yourself exhausted from service as devotion, rather than devotion producing service. When you focus on serving as a result of devotion to Jesus, your outflow is sourced by his renewing presence working through you. As a shadow Christian, you have the privilege of an intimate relationship with Jesus resulting in service extended in his name.

Touch of the Master's Hand

Not only did Jesus allow people to touch him, but he also touched people. By doing so, he demonstrated his desire for intimate contact with his followers. No person was too dirty or too diseased for Jesus. While he could have healed with a spoken word (or a blinked eye, wiggled ear, or pointed finger), he often touched people who needed healing.

Two unnamed blind men approached Jesus and requested healing (Matt. 9:27–31). He asked whether they believed he had the power to heal them. When they said yes, Jesus "touched their eyes" and "their eyes were opened" (Matt. 9:29–30). On another occasion, two other anonymous blind men were sitting by the road outside Jericho. When Jesus walked by, they called out, "Lord, have mercy on us" (Matt. 20:30). After being shushed by the crowd and repeating their cry three times, Jesus approached these men. "Jesus touched their eyes.

Immediately they could see, and they followed him" (Matt. 20:34).

Near Bethsaida, Jesus met another nameless blind man he touched in an unusual way. "Spitting on his eyes and laying his hands on him, [Jesus] asked him, 'Do you see anything?' He looked up and said, 'I see people—they look like trees walking.' Again Jesus placed his hands on the man's eyes. The man looked intently and his sight was restored and he saw everything clearly" (Mark 8:23b–25).

Jesus touched not only the eyes of anonymous people but other body parts as well. On one occasion a deaf man who had difficulty speaking was brought to Jesus. "So he took him away from the crowd in private. After putting his fingers in the man's ears and spitting, he touched his tongue" (Mark 7:33). Jesus prayed a simple prayer, "Be opened!" and "immediately his ears were opened, his tongue was loosened, and he began to speak clearly" (Mark 7:34b–35). Jesus put his fingers in the man's ears and then touched his tongue. Touched his tongue! These were intimate, personal acts.

When Jesus was being arrested, Peter cut off a servant's ear. Jesus touched the bloody mess and healed the man (Luke 22:51). Since this book is about anonymous people and the servant got his name in one of the Gospels (Malchus, John 18:10), he probably shouldn't be included. But a sliced-off ear! That's just too dramatic to leave out.

Jesus touches people—blind, deaf, mute, and bleeding from an ear stub. He wiped spit on people, got earwax on his fingers, and put a finger in someone's mouth. You can't get more personal than that.

There are many other stories about unnamed people touching Jesus, like the woman who touched the hem of his robe (Matt. 9:20–21; Mark 5:27–31; Luke 8:44–48), and throngs of people crowding around Jesus to touch him (Matt. 14:36; Mark 3:10; 6:56; Luke 6:19). Clearly, Jesus is touchable, a powerful demonstration of the intimacy he desires with his followers.

Most people don't mind being touched by an inner circle of family and friends who are emotionally close to them. My adult children hug me when they see me, and my grandchildren crawl all over me. It's natural for families to do this. If strangers or even casual acquaintances tried this, however, it would be uncomfortable. Jesus touched anonymous people to show all of us we are welcome in his inner circle. Shadow Christians are invited there; special status is not needed. You are part of God's family, and like the brother or sister you are, Jesus wants an intimate relationship with you.

It's Going to Be Okay

Jesus also touched his followers to communicate peace, comfort, and support. When Peter, James, and John went up the mountain with Jesus, they didn't know what was about to happen. Jesus was transfigured: "His face shone like the sun; his clothes became as white as the light" (Matt. 17:2). Moses and Elijah arrived to meet with Jesus. Then, God himself spoke from heaven: "This is my beloved Son, with whom I am well-pleased. Listen to him!" (Matt. 17:5). This was too much for the disciples. They "fell facedown and were terrified" (Matt. 17:6). "Jesus came up, touched them, and said, 'Get up; don't be afraid'" (Matt. 17:7). When the disciples (even the leaders, in this case) were terrified, Jesus assured them with meaningful words and a comforting touch.

After his resurrection, he did a similar thing in a different context with lesser-known disciples. When Jesus' followers saw him, they were terrified, thinking they were seeing a ghost. Jesus said, "Peace to you" and then invited them to touch him. He said, "Touch me and see, because a ghost does not have flesh and bones as you can see I have" (Luke 24:36, 39b). Jesus again used meaningful words and a comforting invitation to touch him to bring calm to a stressful situation.

Shadow Christians have the same access to Jesus. When we are troubled, overwhelmed, filled with doubt, or struggling to make sense of a stressful situation, Jesus is available. He touches us with the Word of God, the presence of his Spirit, and the support of fellow believers who become the hands of Jesus. He invites you to touch him by reaching out to him through his Word, your prayers, and your Christian family of supporters. When hurting, you have an intimate Companion who will meet your deepest needs.

First Responders

People who serve and protect, like police officers and firefighters, are heroes in our communities. They are selfless men and women who run toward the sound of danger, even at the expense of personal safety. Taking care of the vulnerable, guarding the innocent, and keeping evil people from running amok is their life's work. They serve with little expectation the people they protect will do anything in return.

When Jesus arrived, he came as a baby. The first responders to his birth showed up when Jesus was most vulnerable. Some anonymous men served and protected him. They guarded him, at risk of their lives, and prevented an evil tyrant from harming him. Their gifts also provided provision for him and his family as they later fled for their lives. These men are commonly called "the wise men" and are only mentioned during the Christmas season. They model what it means to serve Jesus for who he is with no expectation of anything in return. They bowed down to a baby.

Let's bring these amazing men out of the shadows.

The wise men are not only unnamed in the Bible, but their number is also unknown. Tradition indicates there were three, but that's mostly because they brought three gifts. The Bible doesn't say how many there were, only that there were more than one (Matt. 2:1–12). The wise men came "from the east" because they "saw his star" and wanted to worship the "king of the Jews" (Matt. 2:1–2). Their arrival was so consequential that King Herod, secular ruler in the region, heard about it. He summoned the priests and scribes to inquire where "the Messiah would be born" (Matt. 2:4). After determining Jesus had been born in Bethlehem, he summoned the wise men and told them, "Go and search carefully for the child. When you find him, report back to me so that I too can go and worship him" (Matt. 2:8).

The wise men continued their journey, ultimately finding Jesus "with Mary his mother, and falling to their knees, they worshiped him. Then they opened their treasures and presented him with gifts: gold, frankincense, and myrrh" (Matt. 2:11). The wise men were among the first people to worship Jesus. While they may have been somewhat prominent in their home country, their names weren't recorded in the Bible. They represent all people who worship Jesus, not to be noticed or known but because of his unique status. Jesus is our King and we worship him!

Jesus, however, didn't appear very kinglike in this story. He was a baby (less than two years old)—vulnerable, innocent, and dependent on the care of others. The wise men were first responders—among the first to worship Jesus, first to provide for him and his family, and first to protect him. Their gifts included lavish presents inappropriate for a child but convertible to provisions for the journey the family would soon be forced to make. A couple with limited resources was about to flee to Egypt, the first step in a long journey until they arrived at their permanent home in Nazareth (Matt. 2:13–14, 19–23). The wise men's gifts may have sustained the family through upheaval and travels.

The wise men also protected Jesus. After meeting him, they were "warned in a dream not to go back to Herod" so they "returned to their own county by another route" (Matt. 2:12). This infuriated Herod, who, "when he realized that he had been outwitted by the wise men, flew into a rage. He gave orders to massacre all the boys in and around Bethlehem who were two years old and under, in keeping with the time he had learned from the wise men" (Matt. 2:16). The wise men risked their lives to sneak out of town and avoid Herod. His wrath could have, and likely would have, fallen on them if they had been caught. Yet they did what was necessary to protect Jesus. While the ensuing slaughter of baby boys was horrific, Jesus was saved by the courageous, cunning decisions of these men. The wise men served Jesus with no expectation of anything in return.

God could have sent a legion of angels, arranged an army from a world superpower, or struck Herod dead in his tracks to protect Jesus. Yet he didn't do any of that. Instead, he sent a few men, whose names are not important to the story, to protect and serve Jesus. Their example underscores how everyday people know Jesus and serve him. We can easily forget the object of our service and giving is a person—not a program, project, leader, church, school, or denomination. The wise men are also a moving example of serving Jesus because of who he is, not for personal gain. Shadow Christians serve Jesus because of who he is, not primarily because of what he can do for them.

This is a major problem for some believers. They serve Jesus but expect something in return. They pray and expect to get what they want. They give and expect to be rewarded financially. They serve and expect others to appreciate their efforts. Shadow Christians resist these temptations. They serve Jesus because of who he is, not to get something from him.

> **Shadow Christians serve Jesus because of who he is, not primarily because of what he can do for them.**

Jesus wants to know you intimately. Not spotlight Christians but you. He wants you to be close enough to touch. He draws near when his followers, even the anonymous ones, are hurting physically or emotionally. Your identity as a Christian means you are part of his family, not a stranger who needs to keep your distance. Jesus wants an intimate relationship with you. While he is no longer with us in the flesh, he still connects to us through the Bible, the presence of the Holy Spirit, and the support of other believers.

Through Jesus, you know God intimately.

Group Discussion

1. Becoming a Christian gives you a new identity. Are you sure you are a Christian? Why? Ask a few group members to tell their story of becoming a Christian. Pray for every member of your group to be sure of their salvation.

2. Intimacy is a scary word for some people. What does it mean to you? Does the idea of intimacy with God make you uncomfortable? Discuss with your group reasons we are reluctant to experience intimacy with God.

3. When anonymous women touched Jesus, both religious leaders and his disciples became angry for different reasons. Why did these groups react negatively to these women? What social, religious, and moral barriers were broken by these women? Discuss how these problems express themselves today.

4. Read the story of the woman who touched Jesus' robe and was healed (Matt. 9:20–22; Mark 5:25–34; Luke 8:43–48). What can we learn from this woman's example of reaching out to Jesus? What can we learn from the response of Jesus? Discuss these insights with your group.

5. Jesus touched people physically. He doesn't do that in the same way with us, but he touches us through his Word, the Holy Spirit, and fellow believers. Share an example of when you felt "the touch of Jesus" through

any of these means. In what other ways do you sometimes experience Jesus' presence?

6. Some people serve Jesus for what he will do for them. Share an example of when you have done this with your group. Discuss reasons for this problem and ways to prevent it.

7. Ask your group to create a list of ways to serve Jesus without expecting anything in return. Choose at least one way to serve without getting anything in return, and do it this week.

8. God loves us and is affectionate toward us. Do you believe God loves you tenderly? Why is this hard for some people to accept? Discuss reasons Christians struggle to relate to God as an affectionate Father. Pray for insight as you continue this study.

CHAPTER 3

GOD LOVES US TENDERLY

M any people, including some shadow Christians, struggle with believing God really loves them. They project their flawed father-image (often resulting from a bad experience with their human father) on God, envisioning him as a harsh taskmaster or distant demigod they must please at all costs. They find biblical reinforcement by reading their warped perspective into biblical texts about God's wrath. God is holy, no doubt. He is a righteous Judge who holds people accountable for their actions. He has even broken into human history in vengeful ways to annihilate his opponents—actions that point forward to God's promised coming judgment for people who reject him. Scripture passages with these stories and warnings deserve our attention. They are a sobering reminder that God is holy.

While these realities are true, they must be balanced by a parallel declarative statement summarizing another aspect of God's character: "God is love" (1 John 4:8).

God is holy and God is love. He is both at the same time, all the time. That's a mind bender! Those paradoxical qualities are only found in perfect tension and balance in God—never truly emulated or understood by anyone else. The only person who ever combined these qualities perfectly was Jesus, God in human form. Jesus pronounced judgment on religious leaders (multiple stories about the Pharisees) and vigorously confronted hypocrisy (like ransacking the money changers in the temple). He also demonstrated God's love in profound ways as he interacted with people during his time on Earth.

Too often, shadow Christians feel more judged than loved by God. They live with perpetual disappointment and condemnation because of their shortcomings, both real and imagined. They have a difficult time accepting God's forgiveness, focusing too much on their failures as reminders of their inadequacy. They live with a nagging spiritual inferiority complex, made worse by their perceived failures to measure up in our performance-based culture. Shadow Christians have no problem believing God loves others, particularly spotlight Christians who seem to have it all together. Even if they believe God loves them, it's more of a clinical acceptance of a cold theological fact—admitted logically but not embraced or felt emotionally. They have a hard time believing God is their Father who loves them *tenderly*.

That's an unusual word not often used to describe how God relates to us. Yet *tenderly* best describes how Jesus related to one subset of anonymous people during his ministry. Jesus demonstrated tender love by how he related to children, to children in crisis, and to the parents of those children. These stories also illustrate how tenderly God loves you.

Through Jesus, shadow Christians experience God's tender love.

Welcoming Children

Jesus ministered without benefit of childcare to keep little ones occupied (like most global ministry locations today). When crowds gathered around Jesus, children were part of the hustle and bustle. They no doubt behaved like children—pushing to the front so they could see the action, asking questions to understand what was happening, getting distracted and causing commotions, and demanding to be fed or taken to the bathroom. These behaviors are common to children in all cultures; we have no reason to believe things were any different for kids in the crowds around Jesus.

Parents probably wanted their children to meet Jesus. Like today, those parents realized the uniqueness of the moment and wanted their children included. A friend once had the opportunity for a private meeting with Willie Mays and Muhammed Ali—in the same room! He asked if his four-year-old son could have his picture made with this legendary duo. The boy didn't fully understand what was happening at the time, but as a teenager he now has an awesome photo and story to tell. Even more profoundly, parents wanted their children to meet Jesus. What a story they would be able to tell someday!

But the disciples were bothered by the children crowding around Jesus. This was a problem for them. Jesus had been teaching on important and controversial subjects—divorce (Mark 10:1–12, Matt. 19:1–12), prayer (Luke 8:1–8), and humility (Luke 18:9–14)—as people were bringing children to him. These were grown-up issues, not the time or place for children—at least according to the disciples. They felt they had to do something, because "people were bringing little children to him in order that he might touch them" (Mark 10:13a). The Master didn't have time for such frivolous distractions. So they "rebuked them" (Mark 10:13b), acting more like old men yelling, "Get off my yard!" than the spiritually sensitive leaders they were supposed to be. Whatever they said or did, "When Jesus saw it, he was indignant and said to them, 'Let the little children come to me'" (Mark 10:14).

Two things stand out from Jesus' response. First, he was "indignant," which means "agitated, stirred up, or angry." The same word was used to describe the ten disciples' agitation with James and John for asking to sit at

Jesus' right and left hands in heaven (Mark 10:40–41) and the people (disciples and Pharisees) who were angry when a woman broke a perfume jar and anointed Jesus (Mark 14:4). This is the only time the word is associated with Jesus, describing his reaction to prohibiting children from coming to him. Jesus was agitated, even angry, with his followers for how they treated children.

Second, Jesus gave a clear directive: children were welcome in his presence. He wanted them around him. They weren't a distraction or impediment to his ministry. They were, instead, encouraged to come close. When the Bible says, "After taking them in his arms, he [Jesus] laid his hands on them and blessed them" (Mark 10:16), it likely means he let them crawl on his lap and do what children do—squirm, wiggle, and snuggle—while they got acquainted. We sanitize this story by portraying it as a still-life painting with everyone in their first-century Sunday best. It was more likely a sweaty, snotty little mob checking out Jesus with natural curiosity and unfiltered questions. With children in his arms, he showed his followers everyone was welcome to come to him.

Jesus then used this incident as a teaching moment about the makeup of his kingdom. He said, "Don't stop them, because the kingdom of God belongs to such as these. Truly I tell you, whoever does not receive the kingdom of God like a little child will never enter it" (Mark 10:14–15). If the story stopped there, it would be a powerful example of Jesus teaching through common experiences and making a profound point about his kingdom. But then Jesus did something else, a remarkably simple gesture revealing how tenderly he loves members of his kingdom: "After taking them in his arms, he laid his hands on them and blessed them" (Mark 10:16).

Jesus took children into his arms. He cradled the babies, let the toddlers settle in his lap, and caressed the heads or patted the shoulders of older ones. Jesus demonstrated God's tender love by gently touching children, putting his arms around them in a warm embrace. He wasn't a politician politely kissing babies or a nanny catering to the elite. Jesus touched anonymous children, never named but important enough that he rebuked his disciples and demanded they be allowed to interact with him. He was a sanctified Savior but not One so holy he couldn't be touched by runny-nosed, skinned-kneed, dirty-diapered kids. Jesus put his arms around them and pulled them in for a hug.

Jesus loves shadow Christians like this. He said people in his kingdom were like the children in this story. You are his child and you are hug worthy. He tenderly cares for you, no matter how insecure you may feel or obscure your service for him may be. He knows you intimately and loves you tenderly. Jesus loves you so much he takes you in his arms. He provides the warmth, comfort, and tender love you need when you feel most vulnerable.

Caring for Hurting Children

A pediatric hospital is a difficult place to visit. Seeing children in pain and the impact on people who love them is heartrending. When cancer wrecks a tiny body, an infection can't be controlled, or an accident requires reconstructive surgery, the situation is bleak and depressing. When children are in pain, our hearts go out to them. Their pain spreads to their parents and others who care for them in waves of turmoil compounded by feelings of helplessness. Our hearts go out to families and caregivers in these situations as well.

Perhaps you have been one of these children or an adult who loved and cared for one. When our daughter Melody was a junior in high school, she experienced a yearlong debilitating illness. She was a three-sport athlete, playing something year-round. One day, at the beginning of the school year, she came home from soccer practice not feeling well. She went to bed and did not get up for six weeks. It was four months before we had a diagnosis and started a treatment plan. She missed almost an entire year of school and, as a people person, endured a lonely year of isolation during treatments and recovery.

It was a rough year for Melody and the people who loved her. She was fortunate. Her illness abated, and she lives a normal life today. Some aren't so fortunate. We have friends with a daughter who also became sick in high school. She still struggles, almost thirty years later, to manage day-to-day life. A once vibrant young woman, through no fault of her own, has lived with physical pain and emotional suffering for years. It's been hard for her, her parents, and all of us who love her. When a child suffers, the trauma cascades over everyone touched by the situation.

Jesus encountered several families, names never recorded, who had a child in crisis. His tender concern for these anonymous families is another example of Jesus showing love by how he related to children. A boy was feverishly sick, too weak to travel to Jesus (John 4:46–54). His father, a government official in Capernaum, made a trip to Cana (about twenty-four miles) "and pleaded with him to come down and heal his son, since he was about to die" (John 4:47). He implored Jesus, "Sir, . . . come down before my boy dies" (John 4:49). Jesus responded with simple instructions and a promise. He said, "Go, . . . your son will live" (John 4:50). The official started home but was met on the way by some of his servants who told him his son was recovering. When he inquired about the time of the healing, the servants replied, "'Yesterday at one in the afternoon the fever left him.' . . . The father realized this was the very hour at which Jesus had told him, 'Your son will live.'" As a result of this healing, "he himself believed, along with his whole household" (John 4:52–53).

Jesus healed the son of this secular government official, not the favored son of one of his followers. Before the healing, he chided the father, "Unless you people see signs and wonders, you will not believe" (John 4:48). Even though Jesus reproved his listeners for their confused motives, this burdened father wasn't dissuaded. He still asked for and received the healing his son needed. As a result of seeing this sign and wonder, he committed to following Jesus. Jesus tenderly loves people who don't believe in him, who may come to him with mixed motives but are desperate enough to seek his help. You don't have to be a spiritual insider to experience God's tender love.

On another occasion the situation was even worse. Another desperate father came to Jesus with a son who was having seizures because of demon possession (Matt. 17:14–20; Mark 9:14–29; Luke 9:37–43). Matthew recorded the father's plea this way: "When they reached the crowd, a man approached and knelt down before him. 'Lord,' he said, 'have mercy on my son, because he has seizures and suffers terribly. He often falls into the fire and often into the water'" (Matt. 17:14–15). Mark added additional gruesome details: "Teacher, I brought my son to you. He has a spirit that makes him unable to speak. Whenever it seizes him, it throws him down, and he foams at the mouth, grinds his teeth, and becomes rigid" (Mark 9:17–18a). Luke adds another fact, which makes the story even more poignant: the father lamented, "He's my only child" (Luke 9:38). What a tragic situation! As a result of demon-induced seizures, this boy was tossed into fires and streams, foamed at the mouth, ground his teeth, and became stiff as a board. He was his parents' pride and joy, their only child, making their pain even more intense.

When this father asked for Jesus' help, it almost sounded like an apology for bothering him. He told Jesus, "I brought him to your disciples, but they couldn't heal him" (Matt. 17:16). He had tried to get the help his son needed without involving Jesus, to no avail. Jesus' response is a stinging rebuke, which might seem to have included the father. But it was more likely directed to the disciples (for their lack of faith) and the crowds (for their spiritual shallowness). He said, "You unbelieving and perverse generation, how long will I be with you? How long must I put up with you?" (Matt. 17:17). As soon as Jesus learned of the situation, he "rebuked the demon, and it came out of him, and from that moment the boy was healed" (Matt. 17:18). Once again, Jesus showed compassion for a hurting child—after rebuking adults for their spiritual impotence. The contrast is startling: confrontation for bystanders but love extended to a hurting father and a suffering child.

Not much is known about this father, his son, or the unmentioned mother. They are among the anonymous people Jesus encountered and cared for in remarkable ways. He intervened when his disciples were powerless to change the situation. Shadow Christians can depend on Jesus to love them even when others have given up on them.

One final situation was worse than either of these two sick children: a young man had died. Jesus was nearing a village called Nain when he encountered a funeral procession. The dead boy was the only son of his widowed mother. "When the Lord saw her, he had compassion on her and said, 'Don't weep.' Then he came up and touched the open coffin, and the pallbearers stopped. And he said, 'Young man, I tell you, get up!' The dead man sat up and began to speak, and Jesus gave him to his mother" (Luke 7:13–15).

This heartbroken woman was doubly grieved. Her husband had passed away, and now her son had also died. In her culture, most women in this situation would have suffered both emotional loss and financial calamity. Without a man to provide, her situation would have been bleak. Jesus was moved with compassion by her plight and, without being asked, stepped in to meet both her emotional and her practical needs. He soothed her grief and gave her back a provider. Jesus cared enough for this woman to meet her deepest needs, even without being asked.

Jesus cared for this woman as a virtual stranger. He had not yet arrived in town when he saw the funeral procession heading to the burial place. No one introduced this woman to him. She didn't ask for his help. Jesus loves anonymous people preoccupied with their pain and moving through life without him. Jesus still reaches out to unnamed women and men who need his help.

Shadow Christians experience bleak situations and bad days (as do Christian leaders). You hurt deeply because of profound loss. You wonder how you are going to make it through the pain of losing a loved one. You also experience lesser losses—getting fired from a job, a broken engagement, or strained family relationships. All of these circumstances are painful. When they happen, we hurt spiritually and emotionally. Jesus sees his followers in pain and responds, as he did for this woman, by providing emotional support and taking care of practical needs. He strides toward our pain, not slinks away from it. Jesus tenderly touches broken bodies, dying dreams, and fractured relationships with his restorative power.

The Children Effect

Children have an interesting effect on people, including those you least expect to be impacted. Several years ago, a prominent Christian speaker agreed to come to our small church. It was quite an honor for us. His public persona and teaching style were formal and intense. While never harsh, he was well-known for being direct, blunt, and demanding. It was both intimidating and exciting to have him come to our church.

To get the most from the experience of meeting him, we invited him to our home for dinner the night before the conference started. We cooked and cleaned, primped and polished, to get everything ready for our dignified guest. When he arrived at our modest home, I took his topcoat and turned to hang it in our entryway closet. When I turned back around, he was gone! With a rising panic, I looked right, out the door, to see if he had bolted, and then left, toward the kitchen, to see if he had slipped past me somehow. Then I glanced down.

Our nationally known speaker was sprawled out, spread-eagle on his stomach, facing our toddler son, Casey, on the living room floor. He started flapping his arms like a bird and making silly noises, while Casey squealed with delight. Within a few seconds, our son crawled to his new playmate and started pulling on his ears and climbing on his head. I wasn't sure what to do. The last thing I expected at our formal-as-we-could-make-it dinner party was our distinguished guest morphing into a baby-talking climbing toy and being mauled by a drooling toddler. Such is the transformative power of a small child!

Now, thirty years later, my grandchildren elicit the same silliness from me. My now grown-up son Casey, after observing me indulge the whims of my grandchildren, jokingly asked, "Who are you, and what have you done with my father?" Children evoke emotional responses and uncharacteristic behavior, even from those of us who relate and behave very differently in other situations.

Because of my upbringing, my driven personality, and executive job demands, *tender* isn't a word most people would use to describe my relational style. That's not me, unless one of my granddaughters wants to play a game or tell me one of their detailed stories. That's not me, unless I'm wrestling with my grandsons or reading them a book we have already read multiple times. My grandchildren draw something out of me almost no one else does: tender love.

Jesus went out of his way to welcome children and minister to hurting children (as well as the people who cared for them) to show an important aspect of God's love. God loves you tenderly. He has a soft spot in his heart for you. He wants you to get close enough so he can hug you. Pain is like a magnet drawing him closer, not repelling him from you. Jesus revealed God's love perfectly, demonstrating his tender-sided love for his children, including you.

> **God loves you tenderly. He has a soft spot in his heart for you.**

Shadow Christians sometimes struggle to feel loved by God. We are immersed in a performance-based culture that doles out acceptance and accolades based on what we do, not who we are. God isn't like that. He loves you—no matter who you are, what you have done, or what you are going through. He doesn't love spotlight Christians more because of their popularity or accomplishments. God loves every one of his children tenderly.

Will Lamartine Thompson was inspired to become a hymn writer while attending a Dwight L. Moody crusade. He later wrote "Softly and Tenderly," often used as an invitation song after Moody finished preaching. It's so well-known it was sung at Martin Luther King Jr.'s funeral and has been recorded by multiple Grammy and Dove award-winning artists. When Moody was near death, he told Thompson he would rather have written "Softly and Tenderly" than anything he had ever produced. As a fiery evangelist, Moody might not have been labeled "soft" or "tender," yet those were the comforting words that strengthened him as he faced death.

Whether you are facing death or trying to make life work, God loves you. His heart is soft and tender toward you. Jesus showed that aspect of God's love by how he related to children and people who cared for them. If you are part of God's kingdom, you got there by becoming childlike and then becoming his child. You may live in the shadows, but God's love reaches you there.

Through Jesus, you experience God's tender love.

Group Discussion

1. Do you struggle with envisioning God as a loving Father? Why do you struggle with receiving God's love? Discuss with your group how our performance-based culture has infiltrated and marred our understanding of the Christian life.

2. God has tender love for you. Are you comfortable using the word *tender* as one way to describe how God relates to you? Why or why not? Share your ideas with your group.

3. Read these stories of Jesus welcoming children (Mark 10:13–16; Matt. 19:13–15; Luke 18:15–17). Compare and contrast them. What can you learn from the similarities and differences? Discuss your observations with your group.

4. Jesus was indignant with his followers for prohibiting children from coming to him. Why did this make Jesus angry? What does his response teach you about the value of children and children's ministry today? Discuss what this means for your church.

5. What does it mean to become childlike in order to enter the kingdom of God? Why does this keep some people from becoming Christians? Discuss your insights with your group.

6. What is your experience with sick children? What have you learned about God in those circumstances? About yourself? About caring for others? Discuss ways your group can minister to children in crisis and the people who care for them.

7. Google the hymn "Softly and Tenderly." Read the backstory and listen to one of the versions by a popular artist. Why has this hymn been so popular for so long? What part of its message resonates with you? Play it and discuss its meaning with your group.

8. Jesus' actions demonstrate that God knows and loves shadow Christians. What are some other biblical or theological reasons God values them highly? Discuss your ideas with your group. As you move on to the next chapter, ask God to reveal more reasons why he highly values believers who are outside the spotlight.

CHAPTER 4

GOD VALUES US HIGHLY

Some ideas explode in our minds and shape our behavior for a lifetime. It happened to me in a seminary classroom almost forty years ago. The professor said three words, "Theology informs practice." That simple sentence summarized the most consequential lesson from my formal ministerial training. Those words—theology informs practice—mean that what we believe determines what we do (and conversely, what we do reveals our true beliefs). This phrase means our biblical convictions inform personal perspectives, lifestyle choices, and ministry practices. Theological commitments control what we think, feel, and do.

When doctrinal foundations determine perspectives and practices about ministry, we discover an overarching reason shadow Christians are so significant: God highly values what happens outside the limelight.

Because named leaders are featured prominently in the Bible, it's easy to assume they were the only people God used to do his work. But look again. Hiding in plain sight are many examples (featured throughout this book) of the crucial role shadow Christians played in God's story. Just as visible are doctrinal underpinnings that establish and support the important role everyday people have in fulfilling God's purposes.

God highly values what happens outside the limelight.

Why have we missed (or at least minimized) these biblical examples and theological tenets? One reason is we live in an era when popularity equals influence. We follow popular people (like athletes and entertainers) instead of influential people (like teachers and executives). Another reason is natural admiration for superstars in any field. Among Christians, for example, media-savvy pastors of large churches get asked to speak at conferences and lead denominations. Our healthy appreciation for these leaders can morph into a false conclusion that they are more important than people serving in less visible locations and capacities.

Another reason is overfamiliarity with Bible stories and theological concepts. Common assumptions about the content and meaning of biblical passages cause us to ignore details that might influence or even change our perspective.

People who hide things, like spymasters or witness protection program managers, know there are two ways to keep something (or someone) secret. The first is to hide them so well they are virtually impossible to find. Fail-safes and trigger points are built into the system to alert any potential compromise. Most things or people hidden this way are never found.

The other way to keep something secret is to hide it in plain sight. This means making the hidden thing or person a routine part of a community, so familiar they become part of the wallpaper. When a person is hidden this way, no one notices because everyone knows them (or thinks they do). That's what has happened with many shadow Christians in the Bible. Their stories are there, in plain sight, but so familiar we read over the details because we think we already know them.

This is also true of some of the theological underpinnings establishing the importance of shadow Christians. We can parrot the doctrines but fail to understand how significant they really are. We know them so well they lose their impact in our strategic decisions about life and ministry.

Several theological themes in this section establish the importance of shadow Christians in God's kingdom. These may be familiar to you. If so, force yourself to read more slowly and think through the implications.

Remember, theology informs practice. What we believe drives what we do personally and corporately. When theology and practice are disconnected, something is amiss. Either theology needs fine-tuning or our practices need adjusting. This dissonance isn't healthy for leaders or followers. Effective life and ministry are accomplished by doing things God's way, based on timeless truth, not by emulating secular practices, management methods, leadership processes, or motivational techniques. When sound theology informs ministry practice, this overarching conviction emerges: *Shadow Christians are valued by God.*

A Kingdom of Priests

The first theological concept establishing the importance of shadow Christians is the priesthood of believers. Every believer is part of "a royal priesthood" (1 Pet. 2:9), serves as a "priest of the gospel" (Rom. 15:16), and offers "spiritual sacrifices acceptable to God" (1 Pet. 2:5). This doctrine has two primary components, both built on the pattern and nature of priestly work. Priests represent people to God and God to people. They are intermediaries or go-betweens who connect God and people. While "we have a great high priest . . . Jesus the Son of God" (Heb. 4:14), believers still have priestly functions important to advancing God's kingdom.

Every believer is a priest in relation to God, meaning every believer has equal access to God through Jesus.

There aren't categories or rankings of spiritual access to God. Every believer has equal access, can equally represent others before God (through prayer), and has equal standing before God. Some believers operate within an undeclared Christian caste system—acting like there are ranks, levels, or positions that determine spiritual access. But these Christians have completely missed, forgotten, or ignored the priesthood of all believers.

Because of my visible leadership role, people often wait in line after hearing me speak to tell me their story and ask me to pray for them. Praying with people is important, but a subtle assumption underlying this practice troubles me. Their determination to have me pray for them may mean they think my prayers are more effective because of my speaking ability, platform presence, or perceived spiritual insight. My prayer line, however, is no more direct than any other Christian's. Every believer is a priest with equal access to God. The person waiting for me to pray could probably use the time more effectively by asking a shadow Christian to pray for them.

Another aspect of priestly work is representing God to people. Being a kingdom of priests means fulfilling God's purposes. It means communicating to others on God's behalf (sharing your faith), ministering to others (Christian service), representing God in public life (community engagement), and glorifying God in every way possible ("whatever you do, do everything for the glory of God," 1 Cor. 10:31). Being a priest means fulfilling your responsibility as a conduit connecting God with others. This important priestly work isn't reserved for a select few (like it was in the Old Testament). Every believer is now a priest with full access to God and the privilege of ministering on his behalf.

Another related idea is that every Christian is a minister or servant. In the New Testament, *minister* is primarily a verb. In our world, *minister* has become a noun. A minister is a person. To minister, or serve, is an action. The emphasis in the Bible is on the latter, not the former. Because we are a kingdom of priests, all believers are ministers. This means we all "do ministry" to God and others. Shadow Christians are priests and ministers, made so by God, who allows all believers equal access to him and gives all believers the privilege and responsibility of serving others in his name.

> You are a priest and minister representing God to people and people to God.

You, then, are a priest and minister representing God to people and people to God.

Everyone Is Gifted

A second theological foundation for ministry by shadow Christians is every believer has a spiritual gift (or gifts). The

Bible has at least three lists of those gifts (1 Cor. 12:4–11; Eph. 4:11–12; Rom. 12:6–8), although other passages may be included based on how spiritual gifts are understood or interpreted. The number of gifts and their role in the church is debated, but interpreters generally agree on two broad conclusions. First, every believer has received at least one spiritual gift from God. Second, spiritual gifts are bestowed to benefit others. This means all Christians are gifted for service and responsible to use their gifts wisely. It also implies Christian leaders must deploy gifted people effectively to advance God's kingdom. Not doing so undermines ministerial effectiveness and wastes God's good gifts. Leaders must be good stewards of the gifted people God has provided to do his work.

Several corollaries about spiritual gifts among believers make shadow Christians vital to ministry success. First, spiritual gifts are compatible and intertwined. No person has all the gifts necessary for any church or ministry organization to function effectively. We need one another to form a mosaic of ministry impact. Without mutuality among believers, ministry becomes one-dimensional (too narrowly focused) or has many missing pieces (lost opportunities). When we fail to value all spiritual gifts, we miss the blessing of experiencing the panorama of God's grace at work through his followers. We also undermine a primary means of achieving unity among believers. The Bible says: "God has put the body together, giving greater honor to the less honorable, so that there would be no division in the body" (1 Cor. 12:24b–25a).

An effective church worship experience, for example, requires a multitude of spiritual gifts. The more public gifts are on display in the auditorium or sanctuary, but what about the so-called "lesser gifts" active in other locations and ministries? Administrators have assured the facility and other materials are ready for use; teachers are communicating with children in age appropriate classes; mercy-oriented people are caring for infants and toddlers; servants are patrolling the parking lot or preparing people for baptism; and many donors make financial contributions to pay for it all. Foolish leaders focus too much on public gifts and forget to honor the interconnected team that makes it all possible. Most of the gifts in this scenario operate through shadow Christians working outside the spotlight.

Second, all spiritual gifts have value. We tend to focus more on public gifts like preaching or administration. The Bible contradicts this conclusion: "On the contrary, those parts of the body [church] that are weaker are indispensable. And those parts of the body that we consider less honorable, we clothe these with greater honor, and our unrespectable parts are treated with greater respect, which our respectable parts do not need" (1 Cor. 12:22–24).

Several years ago, I had two surgeries to treat thyroid cancer. My parathyroid glands were damaged and stopped working. Afterwards, I had two questions: *What are para-thyroids, and why does losing them matter?*

Parathyroids are four small glands that regulate your body's calcium absorption rate. Calcium is important for bone density but also for nerve transmission (including keeping your heart and lungs working). Suddenly, an insignificant (and heretofore unknown) part of my body became important to me. Because these small glands malfunctioned, I have been taking medicine twice daily for twenty-five years and will do so for the rest of my life. The unseemly parts of the body, and the suppos-edly less important gifts in the church, really matter. We need every person, every gift, fully functioning to have healthy churches, which make a positive difference in our communities.

Finally, spiritual gifts are a source of unity. The Bible says: "Now there are different gifts, but the same Spirit. There are different ministries, but the same Lord. And there are different activities, but the same God works all of them in each person" (1 Cor. 12:4–6). When every per-son's contribution is valued, it produces unity in churches and among Christians. We all sometimes struggle with jealousy, feeling unappreciated, and other self-centered reactions to the successes of others. When these feelings arise, it helps to remember God has gifted each of us to do what he has assigned us and others to do what he has assigned to them. A healthy understanding of spiritual gifts diminishes jealousy among believers. We all matter to God, and when we fulfill our assigned role, we are vital in God's overall plan. This perspective frees us to celebrate the accomplishments of others, even when their accolades exceed what we receive for what we have done.

Every shadow Christian has one or more spiritual gifts. God has included them in his strategy for building strong churches and impacting communities. God allows some to have more public, but not more important, gifts. Part of valuing people serving in the shadows is recognizing the significance of their assignment, thanking God for the opportunity he has given, and honoring God by using our spiritual gifts to do our part.

> Shadow Christians must use their gifts for God's purposes to be accomplished.

Every day, when I take my medicine, I am reminded of the importance of every body part doing its job. Fulfilling God's mission requires more than leaders performing in the spotlight. Shadow Christians must use their gifts for God's purposes to be accomplished.

The Nature of the Church

Another theological tenet establishing the importance of shadow Christians is the nature of the church. The church is a fellowship of believers on mission. Membership is possible because of God's grace, not human merit. The Bible makes this clear: "For you are saved by grace through faith, and this is not from yourselves; it is God's gift—not from works, so that no one can boast" (Eph. 2:8–9). The old saying, "The ground is level at the foot of the cross," is true. Every person comes into relationship with God the same way: by grace, through faith. There's no special status for people based on good works, physical appearance, intellectual capacity, family connections, or even religious devotion. God's grace is the only means of salvation and the only entry point to church fellowship and service.

After underscoring the importance of grace for salvation, the same passage also emphasizes that Christian service is motivated and empowered by Jesus: "For we are his workmanship, created in Christ Jesus for good works, which God prepared ahead of time for us to do" (Eph. 2:10). This verse contains at least two important principles for shadow Christians. First, God has assigned work to every believer. Second, God assigned that work "ahead of time," meaning he has always had a plan to use every person who comes into relationship with him. That's both comforting and challenging, humbling and empowering. It's comforting and humbling to know God has a plan to use you. It's challenging and empowering to know God is counting on you to do your part.

The church is believers working together to expand God's kingdom. Their activities are many and varied, shaped by cultural, economic, and spiritual factors in every community. Shadow Christians are vital to the church's overall impact because they are embedded in every strata of society. They are chosen by God, included in his strategic plan, and empowered for service. This means every believer, including you, can participate fully in God's mission. You have a role to play in God's grand plan.

A Leader's Focus

Shadow Christians are important because of their priestly functions, their spiritual giftedness, and the nature of the church as a voluntary association of equals. Those theological realities reinforce the importance of every Christian serving God and making a spiritual impact in the world. Those doctrinal assertions are true for all believers.

There's another supportive tenet, however, that focuses more on the biblical responsibility of leaders. Their role is equipping believers, all believers, for Christian service. That seems counterintuitive. Leaders are supposed to lead, which usually implies they are doing something significant to advance their organization's mission. We often assume that means they do more than others, do it better than others, and their personal productivity is, therefore, the most important work of all.

That's a misguided understanding of what Christian leaders are supposed to do. Their goal shouldn't be doing more ministry than others or doing it better than others. Their effectiveness isn't measured by personal achievement and resulting accolades. The focus of Christian leaders is equipping other believers for ministry. The Bible tells us God "gave some to be apostles, some prophets, some evangelists, some pastors and teachers, to equip the saints for the work of ministry, *to build up the body of Christ*" (Eph. 4:11–12; emphasis added). The focus of pastors and other ministry leaders, then, is not doing all the ministry but equipping their followers to do ministry, creating strategies to use them effectively, and celebrating their combined success.

This means the ultimate measure of leadership success is how many people are trained, placed, motivated, and celebrated in ministry. For leaders, greatness is measured by their multiplied impact through others, not their personal productivity. Good leaders recognize the multiplying effect of training, placing, motivating, and celebrating what dozens, hundreds, or thousands of everyday believers are able to do, knowing this will always exceed what even the most impressive individual can do on his or her own. Christian leaders recognize the importance of people in the shadows and focus on enhancing their impact.

An Old Testament story (Exod. 18) is one of the best examples of this principle being applied. Moses was running himself ragged trying to solve the legal, moral, and ethical questions and disputes among the Israelites. His father-in-law, Jethro, observed his leadership style and processes. Jethro observed, "What you're doing is not good," and then warned. "You will certainly wear out both yourself and these people who are with you" (Exod. 18:17–18). Notice Jethro cautioned Moses that his leadership style was harming both him and his followers. Trying to do everything damages a superstar leader's health, reputation, and effectiveness. It also frustrates followers who aren't using their gifts, sharing the satisfaction of ministry accomplishment, or growing spiritually by bearing an appropriate burden for their church's ministry productivity.

Jethro gave Moses a recipe for effectiveness. He told him,

> You be the one to represent the people before God and bring their cases to him. Instruct them about the statues and laws, and teach them the way to live and what they must do. But you should select from all the people able men, God-fearing, trustworthy, and hating dishonest profit. Place them over the people as commanders of thousands, hundreds, fifties, and tens. They should judge the people at all times. Then they can bring you every major case but judge every minor case themselves. In this way you will lighten

your load, and they will bear it with you.
If you do this, and God so directs you, you
will be able to endure, and also all these
people will be able to go home satisfied.
(Exod. 18:19b–23)

Good leaders create systems to identify quality people
("God-fearing, trustworthy, and hating dishonest profit")
and place them in appropriate service roles. Some will
be able to share leadership ("commanders of thousands")
while others will take on more personal assignments ("and
tens"). This focus on equipping preserves the leader's
health and increases longevity ("be able to endure") and
lightens the leadership burden ("lighten your load"). It
also has two positive effects on followers: they bear the
burden for ministry effectiveness ("bear it with you")
and their overall satisfaction level increases ("go home
satisfied"). Some leaders mistakenly believe taking care
of every need and meeting every expectation among their
followers are good for everyone. In reality, the opposite is
true. Facilitating a shared ministry environment is better
for everyone.

This means all believers, particularly those who
serve in the shadows, are vital to ministry success in
any church or organization. A wise leader recognizes
this and invests in making everyone, at every organizational level and responsibility, feel like a vital part of the
team. This includes communicating high value for every

ministry role, training people to work to their capacity, acknowledging contributions and rewarding achievements throughout an organization, and resisting the temptation to elevate the importance of your leadership efforts over those of the shadow Christians who serve with you.

In the following chapters, you will meet men and women God used to change their world. They will inspire you to do the same. If you are a spotlight leader, refresh your appreciation for the shadow Christians who are largely responsible for your success. If you are a shadow Christian, keep reading to develop new insights into how to make a difference when no one knows your name.

Through Jesus, you can know God intimately and experience his tender love. Since theology informs practice, you can also know you are highly valued by God and vital to accomplishing his mission today.

Remember, you matter. God chooses and uses people like you.

Group Discussion

1. What does "theology informs practice" mean? Why is it important to base what we think and do on sound theology? Share with your group one way you do this well and one way you can improve.

2. Read 1 Peter 2:1–10. What additional insights can you glean about your priesthood as a believer? Discuss with your group what it means to fulfill both priestly roles, representing people to God and God to people.

3. Read Ephesians 4:7–16; Romans 12:3–8; and 1 Corinthians 12:1–31. What is your spiritual gift? If you are not sure, ask your small group for their help in discerning your gift. Why is every spiritual gift important? Discuss with your group examples of ministry in your church that require a multiplicity of gifts to ensure success.

4. Why is it important to remember every person becomes a Christian by grace through faith? How does this promote equality in the church? Why do we succumb to the temptation to rank some believers as more important than others? Discuss with your group ways to communicate high value to all believers.

5. What is a Christian leader's primary focus? Why do some leaders try to "do it all" in ministry? Discuss with

your group ways to alleviate this problem and help leaders refocus on equipping others for ministry.

6. Besides the four theological convictions outlined in this chapter (priesthood of the believer, giftedness of believers, nature of the church, focus of leaders), can you identify additional theological concepts that support the crucial role of shadow Christians? Discuss your observations with your group.

7. A recurring theme in this chapter is: *shadow Christians are highly valued by God.* Do you agree with this statement? Why or why not? Compare and contrast this conviction to the way the world views people in the shadows.

8. As you prepare for the next chapter, do you think any person can experience God's power? If so, why is this true? If not, why not? Discuss these ideas with your group and pray together for continued insight from this study.

PART TWO

GOD USES
SHADOW CHRISTIANS

CHAPTER 5

WE EXPERIENCE GOD'S POWER

Some people believe God's power is more available to special Christians with better access to God. We debunked this theological fallacy in the previous chapter. But while reaffirming healthy doctrine is essential and foundational, it doesn't always eliminate deeply rooted practices by some believers. Their actions reveal their operational theology (or what they really believe): namely, the myth that some people have greater access to God's power than others. They may also believe this corollary: God only works through special people, spiritual A-listers with most-favored status before God.

Another false conclusion growing out of these misperceptions is the flip side of the coin: believing some people are beyond the reach of God's power. Their sins are so odious, their choices so evil, and their brokenness so devastating that God can't help them. While we celebrate biblical Christians who defy these conclusions, it's hard to believe those same life changes can happen today. Paul conspired to murder Christians (Acts 8:1–3; 9:1–2). Yet God changed him and made him like the people he had previously destroyed. God did that then, and only God can do that today.

Even when we celebrate God's power in and through someone like Paul, we misread his experience by applying it only to prominent leaders like him. There's no biblical or theological reason for that conclusion. Yet many people struggle so profoundly with low spiritual self-esteem or crippling guilt for past failures that they have a hard time believing God's power can work in and through them. These defeatist conclusions undermine the conviction that every person can experience God's power and be a conduit of God's power in service to others.

Shadow Christians experience God's power.

Repeated for Emphasis

Matthew, Mark, and Luke (the first three New Testament books) are sometimes called the Synoptic Gospels because of their similarities. When a story is found in one of the Gospels, it's significant (of course, it's in the Bible). When the same story is repeated in all three of these Gospels, its importance is emphasized. The story of Jesus healing an unnamed leper falls into that category. Here is how Mark told the story (see also Luke 5:12–16; Matt. 8:2–4).

[Jesus] went into all of Galilee, preaching in their synagogues and driving out demons. Then a man with leprosy came to him and, on his knees, begged him: "If you are willing, you can make me clean." Moved with compassion, Jesus reached out his hand and touched him. "I am willing," he told him. "Be made clean." Immediately the leprosy left him, and he was made clean. Then he sternly warned him and sent him away at once, telling him, "See that you say nothing to anyone; but go and show yourself to the priest, and offer what Moses commanded for your cleansing, as a testimony to them." Yet he went out and began to proclaim it widely and to spread the news, with the result that Jesus could no longer enter a town openly. But he was out in deserted places, and they came to him from everywhere. (Mark 1:39–45)

An Unnamed Leper

What do we know about the leper? Most obvious is what we don't know—his name. Jesus sometimes addressed people by name, or his followers noted the names of people he healed (when they later wrote the stories). For example, Jesus healed a blind man named

Bartimaeus (Mark 10:46–52) and called Lazarus back from the dead (John 11:43). More often, however, Jesus healed people who were described but not named. For example, he healed a centurion's sick servant (Matt. 8:5–13), Peter's feverish mother-in-law (Matt. 8:14–15), a paralytic with four friends (Matt. 9:1–8), a hemorrhagic woman (Matt. 9:20–22), and two blind men (Matt. 9:27–31). The emphasis in these healing stories is on Jesus and his power over every kind of ailment, not the identity of the person being healed. The leper's story, and the pattern illustrated by these other stories, underscores a crucial point: God's power is available to every person. His power can touch men and women from all backgrounds with all kinds of ailments, problems, and limitations. No person is too far gone for God to intervene and change them in profound ways.

> **God's power is available to every person.**

Rank has its privileges. Flying close to two million miles on one airline has earned me the highest tier in their frequent flyer program. Elite status gets me various privileges: first-class upgrades, priority rebooking when a flight is canceled, multiple bags checked free, and access to airport lounges. These benefits are privileges. It's easy to forget that and start feeling entitled to them. It only takes one trip on a different airline to remind me. Flying without the privileges isn't nearly as much fun. Being an airline elite is empowering.

Fortunately, rank and privilege can't be earned in God's kingdom and aren't required to experience God's power. Jesus' healing so many anonymous people underscores this reality. His healings extended God's power to needy people without regard for their social standing, financial status, moral condition, or physical abilities. These stories confirm the availability of God's power to all people—no elite frequent flyer status required.

The healing of an unnamed leper illustrates several kinds of people who can experience God's power. Shadow Christians who have similar challenges today can experience God's power. They can also be a conduit of God's power to others who have similar struggles.

Physically Hurting People

The most obvious need the leper had was healing from a debilitating illness. Leprosy was a catchall word in biblical times, describing various skin diseases. Today leprosy is a specific illness (called Hanson's disease), which can be successfully treated with antibiotics. But in the Bible, leprosy referred to all manner of skin ailments (Hanson's disease, psoriasis, shingles, rashes, and other bloody or puss-filled eruptions), none of which were curable back then. These made for a horrible, disfiguring, bleak medical condition for which there was little relief.

Skin diseases of any kind, even those treatable today, are maddeningly uncomfortable. Constant itching and scratching, irritations from clothing, and the pain associated with open sores are all aggravating. Imagine how much worse those symptoms were given the primitive medical care available two millennia ago. When Jesus healed the leper, he gave him immediate relief from physical torment for which there was no other solution.

Despite amazing advances in modern medical care, people still suffer pain from incurable illnesses and tragic accidents. Many others suffer the results of abusing drugs and/or alcohol. Despite treatment plans, pain management clinics, rehab centers, and physical therapy programs, people are still broken by diseases and debilitated by pain. Like the leper, their situation seems hopeless. They are desperate for relief and often call out to God for help.

Should they? Does God still heal people today? Does God intervene to eliminate disease, remove pain, and restore health? Is his healing power available to everyone or just a select few? Does God heal shadow Christians or just the spiritually elite?

The Bible instructs Christians—all of us—to pray for the sick. James wrote, "Is anyone among you suffering? He should pray. Is anyone cheerful? He should sing praises. Is anyone among you sick? He should call for the elders of the church, and they are to pray over him, anointing him with oil in the name of the Lord. The prayer of faith will save the sick person, and the Lord will raise him up; if he has committed sins, he will be forgiven" (James 5:13–15). In this passage, believers are encouraged to pray for themselves ("anyone among you . . . he should pray") and for others ("elders . . . are to pray over him"). Christian leaders ("elders") are responsible to lead in praying for the sick, even though "anyone among you" can do it. There's also a powerful symbol ("anointing . . . with oil") to remind everyone involved that the solution is God's power, not the prayers of any particular person offered in some specific way.

God encourages us to pray for healing when we are sick. He also wants us to pray for other people to be healed. He expects Christian leaders to set an example in this important ministry but invites all of us to join in these kinds of prayers. Most of all, he wants us to remember *he* determines whether and when healing is granted. When praying for healing, it's important to remember God answers *every* prayer. He answers some prayers *yes*, some *no*, and some *wait*. When we don't get the answer we want on the timetable we expect, we mistakenly conclude God didn't answer our prayer. He answered. He said *no* or *wait*. Spiritual maturity is revealed by accepting those answers without wavering in our faith.

God hears every prayer for healing but doesn't always heal every person who asks him or restore every person we pray for. This has always been true, even when Jesus was on Earth. He didn't heal every sick person in the world at that time. But he did heal some! God still heals some people today, including shadow Christians like the woman who told me this story:

> In the summer of 1997, I went on a month-long mission trip to India and Nepal working in orphanages, local churches, and a leper colony. We shared the gospel with people everywhere we went. A few days before we returned to the United States, I got sick. Like really sick. After getting home, I thought, *Since I'm home, I'll start to feel better.* But a week later I was actually much worse. My stomach was cramping so bad I would double over in pain and just cry. My parents took me to the emergency room. After lots of tests, they discovered I had the e-coli virus. It was the same strand of e-coli that had recently killed some people who had eaten contaminated food at a major fast-food restaurant.
>
> The doctors told me there was not much they could do for me. They told me to drink a lot of water, with the hope it would flush the bug out of my system. I did that, but as time went by, I just got weaker and weaker. I couldn't care for myself, so my parents moved me into their

home. I was living on crackers and water and lost over twenty pounds, almost 20 percent of my body weight. When all this happened, I was about to start a new job and was supposed to be married a month later. Things weren't looking good for my health, the job, or the wedding.

Friends and family visited me and sent me flowers and well wishes. Then one evening, some of my mom's friends came to visit. They told me they wanted to pray for my healing. I didn't really want to see anyone since I looked horrible and felt worse. But it was my mom, so I said okay. She helped me into the living room. Her friends anointed me with oil and prayed over me. I had pretty much lost hope by that point, but those ladies hadn't!

After they prayed over me, they helped me back to bed. When I woke up the next morning, the cramping was gone, and for the first time in almost a month, I had no pain. It was completely gone! For the first time in weeks, I wanted more than crackers and water. I wanted some real food.

God used the prayers of those ladies to heal my body. I'll never forget that prayer meeting. Within a week after my healing,

I was able to start my new job (where I have worked for more than twenty years). About a month after the healing, I got married in a wedding that celebrated many things, including my healing and ability to be there that day.

Yes, healings like this still happen today. We can and should ask God for healing and leave the results in his sovereign hands. God decides whom to heal for reasons beyond our understanding.

One thing is clear from the leper's story and my friend's testimony: God doesn't heal people because of their social standing, financial status, or spiritual superiority. He heals all kinds of everyday people. His power is available to everyone, not just those considered spiritually elite or favored. When God answers *no* or *wait* to a prayer for healing, it doesn't mean the prayers were deficient or his power was unavailable to that sick person. God answers prayer—*yes* or *no* or *wait*—for reasons we can't fully fathom. His overarching goal is receiving glory, not giving us what we want or think we need.

When we ask for healing and don't get it, we should assume God wants us to trust his grace to live with our affliction. Like Paul we conclude God wants us to learn, "My grace is sufficient for you, for my power is perfected in weakness" (2 Cor. 12:9). We should never assume God answered *no* or *wait* because we are unworthy of accessing, experiencing, or receiving his power. That's just not true. God's power is available, equally, to every believer—including every shadow Christian like you.

Social Outcasts

The leper also experienced another kind of pain—being a social outcast. The Old Testament (Scriptures in force at that time) had specific instructions for lepers: "The person who has a case of serious skin disease is to have his clothes torn and his hair hanging loose, and he must cover his mouth and cry out, 'Unclean, unclean!' He will remain unclean as long as he has the disease; he is unclean. He must live alone in a place outside the camp" (Lev. 13:45–46). While the physical pain of leprosy was debilitating, being socially outcast because of the disease was disheartening. A leper had to live alone, away from the community, with clothing and a hairstyle warning people of his or her condition. On top of that, a leper had to call out "unclean" anytime a person came within earshot. It was a lonely, miserable way to live.

Imagine living totally alone—never sharing a meal with another person, never getting a hug from a grandchild, never high-fiving after a winning play, never holding hands with your spouse. Totally alone. Imagine never being close enough to another person to have a normal conversation, never discussing confidential matters or sharing intimacies with someone you love. That's how the leper lived. Sadly, there are many lonely people today who feel just as isolated.

Jesus loves social outcasts. If you were bullied in grade school, ignored in high school, and still have a hard time making friends, there's good news for you. If you don't get invited to parties, can't keep up with the latest fads, and feel awkward in social settings, you are just the person Jesus wants to befriend. Jesus loves you, accepts you as you are, and wants you in his family. Jesus wants a relationship with you—just like you are. You may feel like you have been "outside the camp" all your life, but Jesus wants you in his club. Life may feel like a giant middle school cafeteria and you are always eating alone. Jesus wants to sit at your table.

> **Jesus loves social outcasts.**

Jesus feels strongly about having a relationship with you. When Jesus saw the leper, he was "moved with compassion" and "reached out his hand and touched him" (Mark 1:41). The word *compassion*, when used in the Bible, has a much richer meaning than the emotional connotation normally attached to it today. Compassion is often equated with sappy feelings. It's a Hallmark card emotion or a heart emoticon.

In the Bible *compassion* meant to be stirred deeply, to be provoked. It described being motivated by something more akin to anger than sentimentality. Today we consider the heart analogous to emotions and the mind analogous to thoughts, but in the metaphors of the ancient world, the bowels were the seat of emotions and the heart the source of thoughts. In the most literal sense, this word translated "compassion" means being stirred in the bowels—a person was riled up in their deepest being. Jesus feels that way about social misfits. He is profoundly moved by their sense of displacement and wants a relationship with them, so much so he touched a leper! Touching wasn't essential to healing. After all, Jesus raised Lazarus to life by just speaking a few words. Jesus touched the leper for a purpose, to underscore how much he wanted a relationship with him. He shattered every cultural and religious obstacle to cement this relationship. Jesus knocks down the same barriers to connect with shadow Christians like you.

Religious Rejects

Jesus also wants every former outcast to live in a spiritual community, which, updated for today, means a meaningful relationship with a church family. He hinted at this by the final instruction he gave the leper. Since lepers were outcasts from their communities, they were prohibited from going to the tabernacle, the temple, and later to synagogues. They were prohibited from participating in worship services or community religious celebrations.

They were not only social outcasts; they were religious rejects.

Some people feel unworthy of God's love and unfit for inclusion in his community. They wrongly interpret those feelings as evidence God has rejected them. When Jesus went out of his way to heal the leper, he demonstrated how much he wanted a relationship with him. Then, after Jesus healed him, he put the leper on a pathway to reconnect with his community. Jesus did this with some surprising instructions. Jesus "sternly warned him and sent him away at once, telling him, 'See that you say nothing to anyone; but go and show yourself to the priest, and offer what Moses commanded for your cleansing, as a testimony to them'" (Mark 1:43–44).

Three aspects of those instructions are surprising. First, Jesus had just blown away centuries of legal restrictions when he touched the leper. Then he told the leper to fulfill the law. That's an interesting twist in the story. It seems like a contradiction. Why would Jesus set the law aside when healing the leper and then instruct him to fulfill part of the law? Jesus told the leper to fulfill the law required to restore him to his community. He told him this so the community would receive him, not to confirm or validate his healing. Jesus knew the leper needed more than physical healing. He also needed to be restored to his community both socially and spiritually. Jesus wanted to heal him completely, from both physical and relational pain.

Second, Jesus told the leper his law-fulfilling actions would be "a testimony to them" (Mark 1:44). He told the leper to fulfill the law so the community would understand he had been healed and could receive him without reservation. The same thing happens today when Jesus makes a religious reject part of his family. He gives the person salvation and inclusion in his community, the church. This is why new believers who testify of their conversion are enthusiastically received into church membership. Contemporary ways this happens are different than the law required, but the pattern is the same. Jesus establishes a relationship with a person who reports the change to Christians, who then incorporate the new believer into their community. Religious rejects become fellow members of God's family.

Finally, Jesus admonished the leper, "See that you say nothing to anyone" (Mark 1:44). This seems contradictory to Jesus' later commands for his followers to take his message to the whole world. For example, Jesus said, "But you will receive power when the Holy Spirit has come on you, and you will be my witnesses in Jerusalem, in all Judea and Samaria, and to the end of the earth" (Acts 1:8). He wants his followers to "make disciples of all nations, baptizing them in the name of the Father and of the Son and of the Holy Spirit" (Matt. 28:19). Why then did Jesus tell the leper, with the exception of reporting to the priests and offering restorative sacrifices, to keep quiet about his healing?

One creative interpreter suggested, "Jesus was using reverse psychology. He really wanted the leper to tell everyone, so he told him to do the opposite." Seriously? No. Jesus isn't a trickster. The better reason is tucked into the response to the leper's story: "Yet he went out and began to proclaim it widely and to spread the news, with the result that Jesus could no longer enter a town openly. But he was out in deserted places, and they came to him from everywhere" (Mark 1:45). Multitudes mobbed Jesus, who knew they would respond this way—hence the warning. Jesus has always been more interested in devoted disciples than crowds who follow him for what they can get from him. His unusual instructions show the true purpose he had for this healing. He was after the greater good—repentance, faith, and devotion from true disciples. Jesus' instructions were consistent with his broader message and how healings fit into the larger narrative. Jesus healed some people but only as a means to direct attention to his more significant message. The kingdom of God was dawning in their midst, and people needed to repent and believe.

Jesus warned the leper about indiscriminately telling about his healing because he knew what would happen—and did happen. Huge crowds flocked to Jesus. They clamored for him to meet their immediate needs—full bellies today and political power tomorrow—not to become disciples extending his spiritual kingdom. Jesus has never been primarily about drawing crowds. He is and always has been looking for disciples. He has never wanted to be popularized. He wants to be obeyed—radically, through humble service, fulfilling his global kingdom agenda.

Shadow Christians are disciples following Jesus, not groupies shouting after Christian celebrities or peacocks strutting their commitments to impress others. They serve Jesus as resurrected Lord—not a caricatured version of Jesus designed to rally political parties, create self-serving movements, or amass wealth for personal benefit. Shadow Christians value substance over reputation, effectiveness over notoriety. They serve to make disciples, not to draw a crowd, put on a show, or otherwise make a name for themselves. You are at your best when you obey Jesus, not when you do what you think will help him out.

Humble Yourself

God's power is available to anyone and everyone. If you are a religious reject, a social outcast, or hurting physically, God's power is available to you. If you are sick, God may heal you. If not, he will give you the grace to live with your affliction. If you are lonely, God can overcome whatever social stigma is keeping you from him by including you in his family. If you have been rejected, he can embrace you with affection and acceptance. But there is one stipulation. You have to ask him for what you need.

The leper "came to [Jesus] and, on his knees, begged him" for healing (Mark 1:40). He experienced God's power when he asked for what he needed. Two things stand out in the description of his actions. First, he sought help from Jesus. Second, he humbled himself, kneeling and begging, when he asked for help.

The biggest obstacle to experiencing God's power is our pride: "God resists the proud but gives grace to the humble" (James 4:6). Your biggest obstacle to experiencing God's power isn't your lack of A-list status. It's your pride. Dealing with your pride is your problem and yours alone. The Bible never tells you to humble another person, nor does it instruct another person to humble you. Instead, it says, "Humble yourselves" (James 4:10; 1 Pet. 5:6).

> **The biggest obstacle to experiencing God's power is our pride.**

Shadow Christians recognize their dependence on God and reject prideful attitudes and actions that stymie God's power. If you want to experience God's power, humble yourself and ask him for it. Whatever you need God to do or empower you to do, ask him. God wants to work through you to fulfill his mission. He empowers believers who seek him humbly and depend entirely on him. He opposes arrogant Christians who consider themselves God's gift to the world or to the church.

You have a choice. Your capacity for experiencing God's power is more dependent on your humility than on your social standing, financial resources, or religious positions. Will you seek Jesus, kneel down before him, and ask him for what you need? Or will you continue to claim your perceived lack of spiritual status limits your access to God's power? When you humble yourself, you can experience God's power in profound ways that meet your needs and impact other people.

Most of this chapter has been about accessing God's power personally. But shadow Christians know the Christian life isn't all about them. Shadow Christians are channels through which God's power flows in service to others. The following chapters will detail numerous ways this happens. Shadow Christians have access to God's power—both at work in them and for work through them.

You can experience God's power.

Group Discussion

1. Read Luke 5:12–16 and Matthew 8:2–4 and note variations in how the leper's story was told by these writers in contrast to Mark's version. What are some of the differences? Keeping in mind that the authors of the text emphasized certain points of the story that stood out to them, how do you explain the differences? Discuss with your group the significance of the leper's story being in three Gospels (and any insights from the variant readings).

2. Why do some believers doubt God's power is available to them? How do you deal with those feelings? Discuss with your group ways to overcome these feelings of inadequacy.

3. Have you ever prayed for healing? How did God answer your prayer? Do you pray for other people to be healed? Why or why not? Discuss with your group their experiences with praying for healing.

4. Who are the social outcasts in your community? What can you do to communicate God's love and inclusiveness to them? Discuss with your group some strategies to be more welcoming of people from different backgrounds.

5. Why do some people feel like religious rejects? Does your church put up barriers that communicate some

people are less welcome than others? Discuss with your group how you can remove those barriers.

6. Do you agree with my explanation of why Jesus told the leper to keep quiet about his healing? Why or why not? How do believers today serve God for what they can gain from the relationship? Discuss with your group some ways you can avoid this pattern.

7. How can you humble yourself as part of experiencing God's power? Discuss these ideas with your group and pray for one another to develop true humility.

8. Shadow Christians access God's power for personal change and service to others. Before you continue reading, what are some ways you observe God's power working through ordinary Christians to serve others? Discuss these with your group as you prepare for the next chapter.

CHAPTER 6

WE SHARE THE GOSPEL

When God heals from sickness, restores family relationships, provides a new job, or works supernaturally in our lives in some unmistakable way, there's nothing quite like it. It's humbling, awe-inspiring, and invigorating. But there's something even better.

That's when God works through us in another person's life, particularly as we share the gospel and see them saved. Facilitating another person's salvation moment, in spite of our human frailty and spiritual uncertainties, fulfills something deep within us. Being a channel of God's power is even more satisfying than being a recipient of it.

Jesus alluded to this one day when his disciples asked him if he wanted some lunch. He had been witnessing to a woman, too engrossed to stop and eat, when he told them, "I have food to eat that you don't know about" and then continued, "My food is to do the will of him who sent me and to finish his work" (John 4:32, 34). While

Jesus may have meant several things with the phrases "do the will of him" and "finish his work," in this context his primary meaning was telling another person how to trust him for their relationship with God.

Based on Jesus' example, the most fulfilling work any believer can do is share the gospel with another person. It's a soul-satisfying experience, touching us at a deeper place than even satiating physical hunger.

When you are instrumental in another person's salvation, you touch eternity. You connect with God's over-arching purpose in the universe, gathering people for his eternal companionship. Paul described it this way: "This grace was given to me—the least of all the saints—to proclaim to the Gentiles the incalculable riches of Christ. . . . This is according to his eternal purpose accomplished in Christ Jesus our Lord" (Eph. 3:8, 11). There's nothing more fulfilling than being a conduit of God's power when sharing the gospel. His power is available to every Christian, not just a spiritually select few. Jesus said every believer can experience his power for sharing the gospel when he promised, "you will receive power . . . and you will be my witnesses" (Acts 1:8).

While there are many biblical examples of methods and strategies for connecting people with God, it boils down to this: communicate the gospel. Some stories in the Gospels are analogous to bringing people to Jesus. Other times, they illustrate taking Jesus to people. Let's consider examples from both categories in this chapter.

The most important thing to remember, however, is you have been given the privilege, responsibility, and power to share the gospel. When you do, it's likely you will be instrumental in people being saved. Every believer can share the good news about Jesus and be present when someone becomes a Christian. That's God's oldest and best-proven plan for

> You have been given the privilege, responsibility, and power to share the gospel.

getting the gospel to every person in the world. It's also the most exciting spiritual victory you will ever experience.

Shadow Christians share the gospel.

A Spiritual Virus

Gospel spreading is supposed to be a viral movement. In the first century, the gospel traveled person to person as believers enthusiastically shared it with their friends and family. While preachers and church planters were important, the gospel spread most rapidly by word of mouth from believer to unbeliever. By that means it permeated societies and cultural strata in the Mediterranean world, Southern Europe, and Northern Africa. The gospel spread rapidly because everyday believers couldn't stop talking about Jesus—who he is and what he had done for them. Common people were (and are) amazingly effective at introducing people to Jesus.

Jesus' followers were originally called "believers" or "people of the Way." In Antioch they "were first called Christians" (Acts 11:26). Some commentators think this may have been a derogatory title, tagged on early believers because all they talked about was "the Christ." Jesus' followers spoke so frequently and openly about "the Christ," people may have said, "Here come the Christ-ones." Whether it was a positive or negative nickname, it resulted from believers being preoccupied with "the Christ" and earning a reputation for speaking about him often.

This is how the gospel is supposed to be shared—by shadow Christians with friends and family members, not by communication superstars. In the American church (and globally because of the growing pervasiveness of Christian media), there is increasing dependence on attracting people to hear a world-class communicator rather than grassroots gospel talkers sharing with people in their relational circles. Mass methods seem impressive and effective, but are they really? Let's do the math.

The most effective mass evangelist in human history was probably Billy Graham. At his crusade events, about half the attenders were Christians who came to support the event by bringing unbelievers with them. Let's suppose Mr. Graham preached to 100,000 different people in a stadium for ten nights. That's one million people, with half of them likely non-Christians hearing the gospel. That's an awesome accomplishment, which usually took at least a year of intensive preparation.

Now suppose those five hundred thousand Christians had spent the prior year sharing their faith with only one person per week instead of working hard to get one person to go with them to the stadium event. That's not too much to ask, right? Just one person per week? *That's twenty-six million people who would have heard the gospel!* Now let's take it a step further. What if each of those original five hundred thousand Christians who shared the gospel were blessed to see two people come to faith in Christ—only two out of fifty-two. And then let's say each of those two people went on to also share the gospel with one person a week. Before you know it, we're passing fifty, sixty, or seventy million evangelistic encounters!

While huge outreach events have many strengths, they were never designed as God's foundational plan for communicating the gospel to the masses. Simply put, multiplication works faster than addition. God's plan has always been for shadow Christians—not ministry professionals—to share the gospel regularly, consistently, and effectively. When everyday believers do this, the gospel becomes the viral movement it was designed to be.

God wants to use maids and mechanics, truck drivers and teachers' aides, accountants and actors to share the gospel. He is looking for shadow Christians like you to take the gospel to the whole world by first taking it into your world.

A Rose by Any Other Name

Several phrases have been used by recent generations to describe personally sharing the gospel. These change as language evolves, culture shifts, and word usage adapts. Older evangelism training materials refer to sharing your faith as "personal work." This meant more than verbally telling a person about Jesus. This phrase described the entire process of initiating a relationship with someone who needed to hear the gospel, sustaining the relationship by acts of service, continuing the witnessing dialogue over time, and praying for the person until they made a personal commitment to Jesus. This phrase was rich with meaning and foundational for the way many churches understood their evangelism strategy. During my formative years as a minister, an older pastor told me, "Remember, personal work is the key to everything in a church." While he valued preaching, administrating, caregiving, and other pastoral tasks, the conviction he voiced informed how he trained and led others. For him, personal work (leading everyday believers in the continuing task of sharing the gospel relationally) was the key to ministry success.

Another older description of sharing the gospel that has passed out of vogue is "soul winning." That phrase comes from the proverb: "He that winneth souls is wise" (Prov. 11:30 KJV). This verse, in context, has a different purpose than defining evangelism. Nevertheless, the phrase *soul winning* was once a popular description of personal witnessing.

One assumption associated with this phrase is the reason its use has faded. The concept of "soul winning" carries with it the idea of persuasion, a huge turnoff for some Christians today. They wrongly assume persuasion implies putting the hard sell on people to get them to profess faith in Jesus. It also suggests manipulation to some, keeping score to others. Some consider it religiously intolerant or spiritually oppressive to try to "win" someone to any religious faith. Except for a few people who emphasize apologetics and debate the gospel with detractors, many believers resist the idea of persuading another person to commit themselves to Jesus.

The Bible contradicts these conclusions when it advises, "Since we know the fear of the Lord, we try to persuade people. . . . We plead on Christ's behalf: 'Be reconciled to God'" (2 Cor. 5:11, 20). Nevertheless, Christians who share the gospel are seldom called "soul winners" anymore.

While moving away from these phrases, contemporary leaders have coined new ways to describe sharing the gospel. One of these is "lifestyle evangelism." The emphasis in this phrase is sharing the gospel as a way of life, as part of your regular routine. This requires believers to

seize opportunities to share the gospel in daily venues—
at work, at the gym, in a coffee shop, in the bleachers
at a ballgame, on a kids' playdate, or on the golf course.
Lifestyle evangelism emphasizes taking the gospel everywhere and reflects the biblical pattern of gospel sharing.
If believers did this today, the gospel would once again
penetrate every cultural nook and cranny.

What is sometimes missing in this approach, however, is enough emphasis on the second word: evangelism.
Living as a polite, faithful, caring Christian in the midst
of unbelievers isn't sufficient for communicating the gospel to them. You still have to tell them the content of the
gospel.

Some dispute this conclusion and claim the gospel
can be communicated without words. They quote Jesus,
"By this everyone will know that you are my disciples, if
you love one another" (John 13:35). Jesus definitely made
that statement, but how does it relate to gospel sharing? It
says unbelievers will know we are Christians by how we
treat one another. It doesn't say they will spontaneously
conclude how to become a Christian by watching us.
Lifestyle evangelism is a healthy way to describe sharing
your faith—as long as the gospel message is communicated, not just modeled. How you live demonstrates gospel authenticity in your Christian community. What you
say tells an unbeliever how to become part of the family.

Another popular phrase for personal witnessing today
is "gospel conversations." This is another helpful way to

describe sharing your faith as long as conversations lead to presentations. Gospel conversations must include more than spiritual discussions, theoretical questions, or even invitations to church events. They must ultimately include presenting the gospel and asking a person to profess faith in Jesus. Just like "lifestyle evangelism," the phrase "gospel conversations" is a good way to understand personal witnessing as long as the ultimate goal is presenting the gospel, not just having nice religious chats. Conversation must imply and include (maybe after several conversations) a presentation of the gospel.

While the terminology has changed over the years, a better way to saturate our world with the gospel has never been and never will be invented. Changing terminology reflects how every generation finds fresh ways to verbalize its responsibility and privilege of sharing their faith. Whether you are an old-school Christian who does personal work through soul winning or a contemporary believer who has gospel conversations while doing relational evangelism, you are part of God's plan for sharing the gospel. The gospel has always been communicated most effectively when each and every believer is doing personal work to win souls while living authentic relationships and initiating gospel conversations.

Shadow Christians understand this and gladly accept the responsibility. They know most unbelievers in their relational circle aren't coming to their church (or any church), won't call on a pastor with their spiritual questions, and don't know enough about the gospel to become a Christian even if they wanted to. Shadow Christians know their friends and family members are more likely to become Christians if they love them, serve them, pray for them, speak the gospel to them, and patiently work with them until they decide to follow Jesus. Shadow Christians, like you, are willing to bring people to Jesus and take Jesus to people.

Bringing People to Jesus

In the Bible, there are many examples of anonymous believers bringing people to Jesus. One of the most dramatic stories involved four unnamed men who helped an invalid friend drop in on Jesus. The Lord was teaching in Capernaum when "so many people gathered together that there was no more room, not even in the doorway" (Mark 2:2). Four guys showed up, determined to get their friend to Jesus but "since they were not able to bring him to Jesus because of the crowd, they removed the roof above him and after digging through it, they lowered the mat on which the paralytic was lying. Seeing their faith, Jesus told the paralytic, 'Son, your sins are forgiven'" (Mark 2:4–5).

These four men were determined to get their friend to Jesus. They arrived and saw the crowd but were undeterred. They found some ropes, tied them to four corners of the pallet, and hoisted their friend to the roof. They started chipping at and pulling on the thatch, probably causing straw and dirt clods to drop on Jesus and the crowd below. A small hole appeared. They peeked through to be sure they were over the right spot. They enlarged the hole and lowered their paralyzed friend down to Jesus. It's hard to believe the crowd sat quietly during the commotion. What a chaotic scene it must have been! But these men were willing to do whatever it took to get their friend to Jesus. When Jesus saw "their faith" (meaning the faith of the friends and the disabled man), he not only healed the invalid but forgave his sins.

These unnamed friends were the reason this helpless man met Jesus. They went out of their way to carry him to the meeting, risked their safety to get him on the roof, likely endured public catcalls to stop their efforts, and destroyed the final barrier to finishing the job. They were determined their friend was going to meet Jesus.

Shadow Christians do similar things today. They go out of their way to meet the needs of unbelievers, find creative ways to share the gospel with them, serve them prayerfully, and wait patiently until their friends or family members decide to follow Jesus.

Many years ago, a church decided to go out of their way and make a concentrated effort to bring more people in contact with the gospel. They hosted a public opinion poll booth at a regional fair. They built the booth, prepared the survey materials, trained many workers, and staffed the booth daily for more than a week. While wandering through the exhibit building, I came across the booth and stopped to see what it was all about. A booth worker named Burtis led me through the public opinion survey and asked me if I wanted to answer some spiritual interest questions. I did. About thirty minutes later, I had heard the gospel and committed my life to Jesus Christ. As a young teenager, my destiny changed because shadow Christians did something as radical as those guys who removed the roof. They took the gospel to the fair.

But that's not the end of the story.

Burtis became a lifelong friend and mentor. He cared for and served my extended family for many years. He showed up countless times to meet their needs through illnesses, divorces, and deaths. Then, twenty-five years after my conversion, the same man who introduced me to Jesus at the fair helped my mother become a Christian.

> **Shadow Christians work quietly, faithfully, and diligently to share the gospel.**

Shadow Christians work quietly, faithfully, and diligently to share the gospel. They do it in unusual places like rooftops and county fairs. They stick with it, knowing it takes a long time for some people to come to faith.

Who was instrumental in your becoming a Christian? It was likely a shadow Christian who loved you, served you, shared the gospel with you, answered your questions, prayed for you, and then supported your fledgling steps as a new believer. You have the privilege of now doing that for others. Shadow Christians who share their faith are God's strategy for getting the gospel to every person in the world. You are part of that amazing plan.

Taking Jesus to People

Jesus went out of his way to meet an unnamed woman, commonly known as the woman at the well or the Samaritan woman. When telling the story, John wrote, "[Jesus] had to travel through Samaria" (John 4:4). Except, in one sense, he didn't. To take the route he chose, Jesus went *out of his way* to travel through Samaria. "Had to travel" meant it was not the normal route but that he made an intentional choice to go where she was, to meet her on her turf.

Jesus knew a lot about this woman including the time she would come by the well ("noon," John 4:6), her checkered marital history ("you've had five husbands," John 4:18), her current immoral lifestyle ("the man you now have is not your husband," John 4:18), and the curtain of religious confusion she used to justify her behavior ("our ancestors worshiped on this mountain, but you Jews say the place to worship is in Jerusalem," John 4:20). Despite knowing these intimate details, the story does not mention Jesus calling her by name. Yet she is one of the most famous women in Christian history and a timeless example of Jesus going where people were to connect with them.

Once the woman at the well-professed faith in Jesus, she did some things instructive for all shadow Christians—no matter their previous religious beliefs, cultural prejudices, marital history, or moral behavior. The woman "left her water jar, went into town, and told the people, 'Come, see a man who told me everything I ever did. Could this be the Messiah?' They left the town and made their way to him" (John 4:28–30). As a result of her witness, "many Samaritans from that town believed in him because of what the woman said when she testified, 'He told me everything I ever did'" (John 4:39). Ultimately, "many more believed because of what he said. And they told the woman, 'We no longer believe because of what you said, since we have heard for ourselves and know that this really is the Savior of the world'" (John 4:41–42).

Immediately after her encounter with Jesus, the woman at the well went to her village and testified about him. Her story was so compelling people sought Jesus and believed in him. An unnamed woman became the impetus for the good news of Jesus being shared among the Samaritans.

All shadow Christians, not just a spiritually elite few, have the privilege of sharing the gospel with other people. While some will be better at it than others, no one is disqualified because of perceived limitations or past lifestyle choices. The woman at the well had several strikes against her: she was a multi-divorced, openly fornicating, Samaritan woman. That's quite a resume! Yet, once convinced of Jesus' identity, she became a messenger of grace and hope to people who knew her well.

This is the genius of God's plan for sharing the gospel through everyday believers with everyday people. Shadow Christians come from every walk of life with every conceivable sin and shortcoming in their background. Rather than hide those scars and experiences, shadow Christians go among people with similar backgrounds and needs. Bikers go to bikers, executives go to executives, cops go to cops, moms go to moms, and on and on and on. Rather than homogenize believers by leaching out distinctive differences, God uses all kinds of Christians to reach all kinds of people with the gospel.

One shadow Christian is a professional baseball umpire. He has been instrumental in several other umpires becoming believers. Umpires are a close-knit community, a brotherhood with distinctive challenges, expectations, and problems. Only another umpire really understands the difficulties they face both on the baseball field and managing the personal/family dynamics of an on-the-road lifestyle. The best way to reach umpires with the gospel is for a fellow umpire to interface with them. In this case the saying is true: it takes one to reach one.

Can you imagine if a Christian jockey tried to reach umpires? Or if a Christian clown tried to evangelize jockeys? Or if a Christian umpire tried to share the gospel with circus clowns? The gospel flows more naturally through affinity relationships. God uses shadow Christians sprinkled throughout every community among umpires, jockeys, and even clowns. God is looking for shadow Christians who will go out of their way to interact with unbelievers, not shun or avoid contact with them. Jesus modeled this approach. You must follow his example.

"They" Do It

While Jesus was present on Earth, he was generally limited by time and space (his temptation and transfiguration stories are exceptions). Most of the time people had to come to him or he had to go to them for exorcisms, healings, and other miracles. One collection of unnamed servants who helped make these encounters happen is repeatedly referred to as "they" in the Gospels. For example, while Jesus was ministering near Capernaum, "they brought to him many who were demon-possessed. He drove out the spirits with a word and healed all who were sick" (Matt. 8:16). The anonymous "they" brought people to Jesus. "They" might have included the twelve disciples but likely also included a host of other unnamed followers who wanted their friends to receive healing or deliverance. People who had experienced Jesus in some way and had become his followers wanted others to have a similar encounter.

This verse (and most others like it) omits details of these meetings. Have you ever thought about what the details may have been? If we're honest, we tend to sanitize them too easily. These gatherings likely weren't a neat and clean process. Imagine the effort it took to corral and control demoniacs so they could be brought to Jesus. Consider what was required to get large numbers of the sick, disabled, or incapacitated to Jesus. This was no orderly procession of people waiting patiently for their turn. It was more likely a loud, smelly mob scene with "they" doing their best to manage a chaotic, seemingly hopeless parade of pain. But "they" were doing all they could to connect needy people to Jesus.

Reaching people with the gospel is messy. Sinners are sinners and often act like it. Shadow Christians realize building relationships with non-Christians, getting involved in their brokenness, and sharing the consequences of their bad choices is burdensome. But they do it anyway. They are willing to sacrifice personal comfort, get over judgmental attitudes about offensive behavior, and support the wounded as they limp their way to Jesus.

Shadow Christians don't just talk about what it takes to reach people with the gospel; they do it. Shadow Christians like you are the "they" in the gospel-sharing process.

Your Witness Matters

You may devalue your capacity to share your faith or minimize the impact you can have as an anonymous Christian. Keep this in mind: you aren't unknown to the people in your circle of influence. You are likely the only Christian many of those people may ever know. The people at your workplace, in your neighborhood, or at your school may only hear the gospel if they hear it from you. This makes you the most important Christian they may ever meet.

Your witness matters. Maybe you will never preach to hundreds, but you will teach a class or fix a car or bag groceries for someone today. You will share a meal with a family member or meet a friend for coffee. In those interactions you will have the opportunity to talk about your relationship with Jesus, dialogue with others about their religious beliefs, explain how salvation is available through Jesus, and encourage others to become Jesus' followers.

One church celebrates the significance of shadow Christians by having them stand in the water and assist when a new convert is baptized. The most striking aspect of this practice is a different shadow Christian is in the baptistery each time a new candidate is immersed. That's a sign of a healthy church. They aren't depending on a few super witnesses to reach unbelievers. Dozens and dozens of believers in this church are sharing the gospel in their communities. Slowly and steadily, one by one, new people are professing faith in Jesus and requesting baptism. When a shadow Christian is instrumental in leading a person to Jesus, he or she assists with their baptism. Having a different shadow Christian in the baptistery each week is a visual reminder that many different people are sharing their faith and seeing evangelistic results. It's a living example of people coming to Jesus through the work of many, not the efforts of a select few. It also underscores that every believer can share the gospel and be part of its viral movement through a community.

Shadow Christians share the gospel. You can be involved in this awesome privilege. To do so, you must make an intentional, purposeful, determined effort—like taking a roof off a house or going out of your way to meet a woman at a well. Super Christians aren't needed for this important task. Shadow Christians do it best.

You can share the gospel and lead people to Jesus.

Group Discussion

1. Why is sharing the gospel so spiritually satisfying to believers? Ask someone in the group to tell a story of leading another person to faith in Jesus and how it impacted them spiritually.

2. What does it mean for the gospel to "go viral"? What is keeping that from happening in your community? Discuss with your group ways you can encourage one another to share the gospel more often and more effectively.

3. What are some positive and negative aspects of these descriptions of sharing the gospel (personal work, soul winning, relational evangelism, gospel conversations)? Discuss them with your group.

4. Read John 4:1–42 and Mark 2:1–12. What demonstrates intentionality in connecting people to Jesus? What demonstrates urgency? What demonstrates focus? Discuss with your group ways you can be more intentional, urgent, and focused on sharing the gospel.

5. Why is gospel sharing by every believer God's plan? Discuss with your group some reasons why this plan is so strategic for the global church. What is limiting you from doing your part in fulfilling God's plan? How will you change?

6. Read Ephesians 3:8. How does Paul's claim to be the "least of all the saints" eliminate excuses believers use to disqualify themselves from sharing the gospel with others?

7. What does your church do to encourage and recognize believers who regularly share the gospel? Besides the baptism story in this chapter, what else can your church do to magnify the role of shadow Christians in people coming to faith in Jesus? Discuss with your group how to suggest these ideas to church leaders.

8. Shadow Christians do more than share the gospel. They also serve churches and ministries in many other ways. As you prepare for the next chapter, discuss with your group some of the ways shadow Christians serve in your church and why their contribution is so important.

CHAPTER 7

WE ARE THE MINISTRY WORKFORCE

Most churches and ministries have an organizational chart or "org chart" for short. They contain the names of employees or volunteers, at least the directors or managers in large organizations, who form the operational team that gets the work done. One box at the top of the chart is usually reserved for the overall leader—pastor, president, or executive director. The person in the top box has the biggest office, receives the largest salary, is well-known throughout the organization, and may have a public following. Top-box people are important. They cast vision, enforce mission discipline, handle public relations, avoid legal entanglements, ensure fiscal viability, and make decisions affecting everyone else on the chart. These spotlight leaders are often celebrated and credited with organizational success.

True ministry effectiveness, however, is determined more by the people in the boxes cascading down the chart than the top-box leaders. In churches most of these people are volunteers serving after they have completed a full workweek and taken care of normal life responsibilities. In organizations these rest-of-the-boxes people have smaller work spaces, make less money, have more limited authority, and aren't well-known outside the organization, yet they serve with quiet devotion. Whether volunteers or employees, these shadow Christians accomplish the organization's mission by staying on task and doing their job. They are an important cog in the machine, doing their part to complete the detailed work required in every church or ministry.

These shadow Christians can be divided into two loosely defined groups. Some have leadership responsibilities scaled to the available time and talent of the person in the role. Others are workers, people lower on the chart who focus entirely on the tasks at hand. Sometimes, particularly in smaller churches or organizations, these distinctions are blurred. But in every setting these leaders/workers are the implementers who get the work done. Even though they serve in obscurity, they draw deep satisfaction from being part of a larger mission and vision. They value their role and strive to ensure overall organizational health. Without them nothing consequential happens.

Shadow Christians are the ministry workforce.

Kingdom Inc.

If there had been an org chart when "Kingdom Incorporated" was a start-up, it would have looked like this. Jesus was in the top box. He was definitely in charge. The next level had three boxes occupied by Peter, James, and John. A case could be made that Peter's name should have been in a shaded or slightly larger box since he was recognized as a leader among this inner core. The next level of the chart was the other nine named disciples. They were placed in leadership but at a lower level than Peter, James, and John.

All these men are named leaders. They are famous (infamous in the case of Judas) in history. Some of their remarkable feats are described in the Bible, others in Christian history. They have churches and schools and religious orders named after them. In some traditions they are called saints. People venerate them, even to the point of praying to them or ascribing spiritual power to their likeness or relics. They are quintessential spotlight leaders, not shadow Christians.

The next level on the Kingdom Inc. org chart shifts the focus. We are introduced to the next wave of workers when "the Lord appointed seventy-two others, and he sent them ahead of him in pairs to every town and place where he himself was about to go" (Luke 10:1). Jesus selected seventy-two followers and sent them to do his work. He then described what they were supposed to do, summarized by these key words.

Pray. "The harvest is abundant, but the workers are few. Therefore, pray to the Lord of the harvest to send out workers into his harvest" (Luke 10:2).

Trust. "Don't carry a money-bag, traveling bag, or sandals; don't greet anyone along the road" (Luke 10:4).

Bless. "Whatever house you enter, first say, 'Peace to this household.' If a person of peace is there, your peace will rest on him; but if not, it will return to you" (Luke 10:5–6).

Reside. "Remain in the same house, eating and drinking what they offer, for the worker is worthy of his wages. Don't move from house to house. . . . Eat the things set before you" (Luke 10:7–8).

Heal. "Heal the sick who are there" (Luke 10:9a).

Witness. "And tell them, 'The kingdom of God has come near you'" (Luke 10:9b).

Warn. "When you enter any town, and they don't welcome you, go out into its streets and say, 'We are wiping off even the dust of your town that clings to our feet as a witness against you'" (Luke 10:10–11a).

Pray, trust, bless, reside, heal, witness, and warn were items on their job description. Jesus then predicted coming judgment on several cities that would reject these messengers. He concluded by reminding them, "Whoever listens to you listens to me. Whoever rejects you rejects me. And whoever rejects me rejects the one who sent me"

(Luke 10:16). Their assignments were hands-on ministry tasks, not managing others who did the work. They were promised their work would be challenging, rife with difficulty, and met with opposition. These weren't cushy management positions. They were line jobs in ministry production.

These kingdom workers were vital for expanding Jesus' ministry and connecting his mission to a larger audience. But were they really? Jesus had the power to communicate his message to everyone in the world while simultaneously healing every sick person, feeding every hungry person, and housing every homeless person. He had the power but chose not to use it to produce instantaneous results. Instead, he selected twelve named disciples and seventy-two anonymous associates to start the process of expanding his kingdom around the world.

> **Jesus' strategy depends on using everyday people to get his work done.**

In the beginning, Jesus' strategy depended on using everyday people to get his work done. It still does. That's why he chose you.

Followers Are Vital

One good definition of leadership is: "Leadership is an influence relationship among leaders and followers who intend real changes that reflect their mutual purposes."[2] A team of academic researchers developed this definition based on a comprehensive study of how leadership had been defined throughout the twentieth century. It touches on the key components of leadership and brings them into balance in one cogent statement.

One of the strongest aspects of this definition is its emphasis on the importance of followers in the leadership equation. In fact, that phrase in the definition has grown more prominent in my understanding of leadership over the years: "among leaders and followers." This phrase indicates that leadership happens within relationships. It involves interaction among people committed to "mutual purposes," as the definition concludes. The phrase means leadership takes place when leaders and followers are both relationally engaged and operationally active. This is a vital distinction from how many people perceive leadership. They mistakenly believe leadership is something one person does to another person or group. This definition emphasizes leadership as an outcome between interconnected people, not a set of actions a leader does to followers.

As already mentioned, there are gradations of responsibility among leaders and followers in churches and ministry organizations. In other words, some followers are also leaders (just on a smaller scale than other leaders with the broadest scope and influence). Some leaders are also followers, depending on where they are placed in the org chart. Leadership, as an outcome, happens when leaders, leader/followers, follower/leaders, and followers are all working together in dynamic synergy.

This emphasis on defining followers to include layers of leaders is in line with Jesus' example. He chose eighty-four people to be on his team and sent them to work on his behalf. He trained them, equipped them, and supported them. Ultimately, he trusted them to carry his kingdom message to the multitudes. While Jesus could have expanded his kingdom by any supernatural means, he rejected those strategies in favor of what seems like a more pedestrian approach. He used people—top leaders, support leaders, and field workers—to get his work done.

Followers Who Lead

Shadow Christians occupy leadership roles on the org charts in most churches and ministries. They also take on the working roles that make organizations operational, including coordinating and supervising other volunteers doing hands-on ministry. In churches, shadow Christians serve as children's ministry coordinators, vacation Bible school directors, worship leaders, and head ushers. These workers might be called "ministry managers" since they fill the middle management roles in churches. Other ministry organizations have program managers, executive assistants, and department directors—some compensated, others working as volunteers. The people in these roles are the operational backbone of churches and ministry organizations.

During my tenure as executive director of the Northwest Baptist Convention (Washington, Oregon, and Northern Idaho), a man moved from Texas to be an area leader coordinating the ministry of a significant number of churches. He had previously led a similar ministry in Texas that included consulting with churches and mentoring pastors. After working in the Northwest for three years, he told me: "The difference between the churches in Texas and the Northwest isn't the quality or commitment of the pastors. It's the number of lay leaders in the churches." He continued, "In Texas, Christian colleges and Christian ministries at secular universities have been turning out teachers, coaches, doctors, nurses, attorneys, engineers, and architects for generations. They have joined churches, taken on leadership and service roles, given tithes and offerings based on earnings from solid jobs, and helped pastors build strong churches. That's been going on for about 150 years, and it's why Texas churches are so much stronger than those out here. Churches in the Northwest are still developing their lay leadership base."

His comments clarified an important distinction between two different ministry fields, one known for strong churches and the other still working to build more of them. The difference wasn't the quality of the person in the top box but the scarcity of effective leaders and workers to fill out the rest of the org chart.

This doesn't demean effective Christians serving in Northwest churches. The quality of their service is outstanding. The issue is quantity, not quality. Colleges and student ministries were producing lay leaders in Texas (and other parts of the Bible Belt) for decades before the Northwest Baptist Convention formed in 1948. Some regions in the United States have a 150- to 200-year head start on building the lay support base churches in the Northwest (and other less Christian regions) are still developing. This is a microcosm of what happens any place in the world the gospel is planted. A missionary or church planter (top-box person) arrives and starts the movement. But sustainability isn't achieved until Christians emerge in such strength that they provide the base upon which indigenous churches can be built. Strong churches and ministry movements are sustained and expanded by the people who fill various roles on the org chart.

That's My Ministry

When shadow Christians step into these roles in a church, they lose some of their anonymity. They become more well-known in their ministry setting. They become directors or coordinators or workers who fulfill an important role for the people they lead. But even with that bit of notoriety, they are still largely unknown outside their church.

What motivates people to take on these roles and become such vital kingdom workers? It's not the money (there isn't any involved) or the accolades (not usually more than an occasional compliment). People take on these leadership roles because they have a strong sense that it's what God wants them to do. Many even express this as responding to God's call, meaning he has called them to ministry leadership, and they have accepted their particular assignment. Some of my favorite shadow Christians over the years have answered the question of why they serve by saying, "Because that's my ministry."

"That's my ministry" expresses a certainty of purpose, an appropriate sense of ownership, and a perspective of serving in response to God's initiative. It may sound possessive or presumptive to some, but those faulty conclusions would mortify most people making this claim. They have a healthy awareness of their inadequacy and marvel that God has given them their role—in fact, any role—in his plan. Their emphasis on "my" speaks more of the responsibility they feel for their assignment than pride of owning their role. They have come to a conviction about their part in God's plan and devote themselves to getting it done.

Consider E. Y. Washam. He was convinced boys needed someone who cared for them and would teach them the Word of God. He taught sixth graders, and I was one of them. He wore Coke-bottle-bottom glasses (made his eyes look like they were bugging out) and read the Sunday school quarterly to us each week. That was his teaching method. It was boring, to say the least. So, why did we show up week after week? Because Brother Washam (as we called him back in the day) cared about us and was committed to us. He came by my house every few weeks to check on me. Since no one else in my family went to church, his visits were a lifeline of support. He also invited boys to his home, where his wife served puffy marshmallow treats, and we watched college football or worked on a craft or played a game in his backyard. He prayed for us and showed us God's love in practical ways. He was a retired carpenter who led a church's work with sixth-grade boys for years because, as he would say, "That's my ministry."

A few years later as an associate pastor, I was honored to lead a prayer at this good man's memorial service. Because he was a shadow Christian, only his closest church friends and a few family members attended his service. His care for me, despite his limited teaching ability, helped produce a seminary president who hopefully uses more effective teaching methods but will never approach Brother Washam's personal concern for the people he taught. That's the impact you can make as a shadow Christian who says, "That's my ministry."

Rick directs a men's ministry at his church involving about eighty men. He has nursed it from a small group to an influential force. Sheila has led youth ministry her entire adult life. She sometimes thinks she is getting too old to be relevant, but the cluster of girls gathered around her each Sunday indicates otherwise. Ann has worked in preschool or children's ministry for about forty years. Her heart is with little ones who need foundational instruction in God's Word. All of these people have told me, at one time or another, they do what they do because "that's my ministry." They have a sense of calling and obligation, coupled with a humble determination to do their part to advance God's kingdom. You have the same privilege and responsibility to find your role on the org chart and fulfill it.

Finding Your Spot

Shadow Christians who take on leadership or service roles in churches and ministry organizations aren't seasonal workers who commit for a month or to support an event. They settle in and stay a while. They invest training time learning necessary skills to do their job and hang tough through discouraging, difficult challenges. Because they serve in response to God's call, they are committed for the long haul, not until someone else comes along who will take over for them. Their expertise becomes an asset for building a strong ministry. Their value increases over time as they accumulate skills, experiences, and lessons learned the hard way. Their longevity becomes foundational to prolonged ministry success. Building strong ministries takes time. Tenured workers help make it happen.

If you are a shadow Christian who needs to find a place to serve, a role you can call "my ministry," work through these steps.

First, ask God to guide you. He wants to use you more than you want to be used, so you can count on him to answer this prayer. Be alert to invitations or possibilities God brings to your awareness. Pray and expect an answer.

Second, look for a ministry opportunity that matches your gifts, skill set, personal interests, and life experiences. If you are naturally gregarious, join the greeting team. If you enjoy compassionate interaction with hurting people, help with benevolence ministries. If instructing others is your passion, discover your church's path to becoming a teacher and get started. If you are a born organizer, find a ministry leader who needs an assistant.

Many people fail to realize ministry roles usually flow out of their gifts, skills, interests, and experiences. God made you with certain characteristics, and you have developed other qualities over the years. Don't wrongly assume those are irrelevant to finding your ministry. Recognize them as guide stones. Some of the unhappiest Christians are those serving where they don't fit. This is different from serving in a difficult setting. Everyone involved in ministry work has problems at one time or another. When you are miscast, however, trying to do something for which you aren't really suited, you will be unhappy (and so will the people around you).

One friend loved teaching children and did it well. Over time she was asked to lead the children's ministry in her church. It thrived until it grew to the place she no longer had any contact with children. She spent all her time training, motivating, and troubleshooting with adult volunteers who actually worked with kids. She finally resigned saying, "God called me to work with children, not manage a children's ministry." She returned to teaching in a classroom, and her ministry joy was restored.

Third, be willing to start small, to take one of the boxes at the bottom of the chart. Ask God where he wants you to serve. Make the best decision you can based on your abilities and interests. Then accept the role God and others give you. Don't be upset if you are given a small role. God may be testing your character and shaping your skills for larger challenges later.

For ten years, I was the chaplain of a Major League Baseball team, which involved thousands of hours in personal ministry from hospital rooms to World Series-winning clubhouses. It was an honor and a privilege. People often asked me, "How did you get that job?" My answer, "For about fifteen years, before I was asked to work with Major Leaguers, I was the self-appointed chaplain to a local Little League." I was the only one who knew about the appointment, but I was sure God gave me the assignment to minister in that setting. God saw that

I was faithful in a small thing, and he gave me a larger opportunity (Matt. 25:14–30). Some people want God to give them a top-box job, a position in the spotlight. God usually starts people in the shadows and leaves most people there. Choose to obey God in the assignment he gives and trust him to promote you as he desires, not as you demand.

Shadow Christians fill out the org chart in every church and Christian organization, doing the hands-on tasks required in every ministry setting. Some may rise to leadership roles, but that's not their goal. They are content to find their role and fulfill it, perhaps for decades. They are committed to fulfilling God's mission and the vision of their top-box leader. Shadow Christians like you take on the roles necessary to make sure the work gets done.

You are the ministry workforce. Find your role and start serving.

Group Discussion

1. Read Luke 10:1–12. Why did Jesus choose anonymous workers and send them out to expand his kingdom? How did this establish a pattern for today? Discuss with your group how to apply this pattern in your ministry setting.

2. Do you agree with the emphasis on followers in the definition of leadership in this chapter? Why or why not? Do you agree that leadership is a relationship between people, or do you define leadership as something one person does to another person or group? Why or why not? Discuss your ideas with your group.

3. Ask someone in your group to share an example of a shadow Christian leader or worker who positively impacted them. Discuss with your group what you can learn from this person's example.

4. Ask someone in your group to share an example of a current person who models what it means to "find your ministry." Discuss with your group what you can learn from this person's example.

5. Do you believe God wants you to accept a leadership role in your church or a ministry organization? If so, what is holding you back? Discuss these barriers with your group and pray with them for a breakthrough.

6. Do you believe God wants you to take on a service role in your church or a ministry organization? Which of the following suggestions do you need to heed most right now (pray about it, find a role compatible with who you are, and be willing to start small)? Discuss your conclusion with your group and ask for their input into where you might serve most effectively.

7. Read Matthew 25:14–30. What does this story teach you about leadership roles in God's kingdom? Share your insights and discuss them with your group.

8. As you continue this study, is there any job in Christian service you would not consider doing? Why or why not? Pray with your group about the role God wants to assign to each person.

CHAPTER 8

WE DO THE DIRTY WORK

Someone has to change nasty diapers and clean up vomit. When our children were younger, we had our share of handling both eruptions. My wife is a super-mom (and an early childhood education specialist) who loves preschool children and probably knows as much about them as anyone. Even so, for some reason, vomit was her Kryptonite. She changed thousands of diapers, but when one of our children heaved, she vacated the premises and sent me in as the hazmat crew. We were a compatible cleanup couple, it turns out, since the diapers were worse to me. So we made a deal. Ann would take care of most of the diapers if I handled the stomach pro-jectiles. Too much information? Maybe, but that's real life. Someone in every family, and every church or minis-try, does the dirty work.

Someone provides child care, fills up the baptistery, mows the lawn, takes out the trash, folds bulletins, enters financial information, keeps attendance records, cooks meals, buses tables, patrols the parking lot, drives the church van, counsels at youth camp, and sorts out fights on the preschool playground. As described in the last chapter, some shadow Christians take on leadership or service roles, which show up on an org chart. But even deeper in the shadows are believers who do these dirty jobs. They are the foot soldiers, the boots on the ground, that make hands-on ministry actually happen. They fix the messes, solve the problems, and take care of the details no one else notices.

These servants specialize in meeting ministry needs others either fail to notice or allow to fall through the cracks. They aren't looking for jobs others consider important. They prefer doing things no one else wants to do, often in out-of-the-way places without fanfare. They take on important tasks others overlook, no matter how insignificant they may seem.

When coaching Little Leaguers, I would ask them, "What's the most important position on the team?" They would usually reply pitcher, catcher, or shortstop. The right answer was, "The position you're playing." A team depends on every person doing their job, in the moment they are involved in a play, to be successful. Churches and ministry organizations are the same. On Sunday morning the senior pastor matters, but so do parking lot greeters and childcare providers. Each person must fulfill their role for ministry efforts to succeed. Every job matters, including those considered menial or tedious and done behind the scenes by unnamed believers.

Shadow Christians do the dirty work.

Providing Hospitality

She was sick, bedridden with a high fever, too ill to meet Jesus when he arrived in her hometown. Her son-in-law (Peter) was one of Jesus' followers, a rising leader in his kingdom movement, so Jesus stayed at Peter's house. When Jesus arrived and found Peter's mother-in-law lying in bed, "he touched her hand, and the fever left her" (Matt. 8:15a). What a great moment that must have been! It deserved a big celebration, but that's not what happened.

Peter's mother-in-law, known in history by her family title but not her name, "got up and began to serve him [Jesus]" (Matt. 8:15).

The details of her service aren't included in the story, but a phrase in the narrative hints at what it might have been. After staying at Peter's house throughout the day, "when evening came" (Matt. 8:16) Jesus continued his ministry by performing exorcisms and healings. The demands of his evening ministry suggest Peter's mother-in-law served Jesus by providing meals and a place for rest during the day. Her hospitality helped prepare him for a long night of ministry encounters. This unnamed woman got up from her sickbed to serve Jesus. She made sure he had food to eat, something to drink, and a comfortable place to rest. After being healed, she didn't go on the speaking circuit describing her miraculous recovery. She went to the kitchen.

Inez was in her seventies when she and her husband, Glenn, learned about a church being planted in their area. They were old-school Baptists; hymns and the King James Version were their staples. Yet they also had a Baptist heart for reaching people with the gospel. Inez told me, "We want to help build a church to reach young families." They joined our contemporary church to serve, not to be served. During worship services, they would stand silently when everyone else sang worship songs. They weren't protesting; they just didn't know the newer songs. But Inez had a skill set and passion every generation appreciates. She knew how to cook, how to organize events that included meals, and how to make sure everyone had a good time. For several years, until she couldn't physically do it any longer, she coordinated the hospitality ministry of our growing church. Younger women eventually took over her role but only after learning from Inez's example of the importance of hospitality.

Shadow Christians set up the tables, install the décor, prepare the food, serve the meals, wash the dishes, mop the floor, and haul out the trash. The rest of us enjoy the benefits of their hard work making hospitality events happen, like Peter's mother-in-law and a shadow Christian named Inez.

Protective Services

Sadly, one of the needs in churches and ministry organizations today is protective services. This takes many forms. Some prominent leaders need personal protection ranging from armed guards to plainclothes companions who watch over them and their families while they are in public. Many churches have parking patrols to protect vehicles from being burglarized during worship services. Some organizations have video surveillance, monitored in real time, to detect threats in and around their facilities. Most churches have some type of check-in system for children and a screening process for members who work with minors. While in a few cases security professionals oversee all this, most churches use a cadre of volunteers as their security force. They are the unseen shield protecting others from threats to their well-being, property, or, in rare cases, life.

Shadow Christians protecting ministry leaders and the churches/organizations they lead have been part of Christianity since its beginning. When Paul first became a Christian, he started his public ministry in Damascus. It wasn't long before "the Jews conspired to kill him" (Acts 9:23). They organized an assassination attempt, "watching the gates day and night intending to kill him" (Acts 9:24). As soon as Paul showed himself in the most public place (the gates), henchmen intended to murder him and thus deter anyone else from preaching about Jesus as the Messiah.

Some shadow Christians decided to intervene. These unnamed protectors "took [Paul] by night and lowered him in a large basket through an opening in the wall" (Acts 9:25). Paul then fled to Jerusalem, met Barnabas, communicated his conversion story to the Jerusalem church, and once again experienced conflict with the Jews. They also "tried to kill him" (Acts 9:29). A second group of anonymous Christians intervened and "took [Paul] down to Caesarea and sent him off to Tarsus" (Acts 9:30). He remained there until Barnabas brought him to Antioch to become part of their leadership team (Acts 11:25–26).

Paul later found himself in other life-threatening situations recorded in Acts. In some cases, fellow believers looked out for him. In other instances, Roman authorities protected him. One unnamed young man, however, deserves to be singled out.

Paul was in prison when "the Jews formed a conspiracy and bound themselves under a curse not to eat or drink until they had killed Paul. There were more than forty who had formed this plot. These men went to the chief priests and elders and said, 'We have bound ourselves under a solemn curse that we won't eat anything until we have killed Paul'" (Acts 23:12–14). These vigilantes told the chief priests and elders to "make a request to the commander that he bring him [Paul] down to you as if you were going to investigate his case more thoroughly. But, before he gets near, we are ready to kill him'" (Acts 23:15).

The son of Paul's sister (his nephew) heard about the ambush. He reported it to Paul, who then asked one of the Roman centurions guarding him to take the "young man to the commander" (Acts 23:17). This courageous boy conveyed the ambush details to the Roman officer in charge of Paul's imprisonment. He summoned two hundred soldiers, two hundred spearmen, and seventy mounted cavalrymen as a protective escort to transfer Paul to Caesarea (Acts 23:23). He was moved successfully, and those fellows who had sworn to a hunger strike had a long, ravenous wait. This unnamed nephew showed remarkable resolve in the face of personal danger. He risked his life by revealing the ambush plot and reporting it to a Roman officer. His actions saved Paul's life. Subsequently, Paul extended his teaching ministry to Rome and wrote several letters that comprise much of the New Testament.

A younger shadow Christian was the means for delivering Paul from certain death, centering the Christian message in the capital of the Roman Empire, and producing a significant portion of the New Testament. God uses some people to protect others. While the protectors usually remain anonymous, the protected are freed to extend God's kingdom unencumbered by worries about personal safety. While Paul is a towering figure in Christian history (very much a spotlight leader), his life, latter ministry, and instruction to us through his writings were made possible by his nephew, an unnamed boy serving in the shadows.

"We Do What's Next"

A few years ago, an opportunity to help plant a church included remodeling an older church building. The first step was demolition of the out-of-date portion of the facility. A friend received a long email explaining the situation and asking if he wanted to join the mission trip team. He wrote back one sentence: "You had me at demo." Some people find it fun to swing a sledgehammer and crush things!

This team did the dirty work—pulling broken toilets, scraping up ancient carpet, knocking down walls, and hauling it all away. Their work paved the way for the visible improvements to come. Some people told them, "Sorry this is such a nasty project. We wish someone else could have done it." The team didn't see it that way. It had to be done, so they got it done.

Another volunteer mission group had a similar experience. They reported for work on a building project and asked, "What's next?" The foreman replied, "Well, it's a dirty job, and I hate to ask you to do it." He needed insulation stapled into a gabled ceiling in a large auditorium in 100-plus degree conditions. The team leader replied, "We came to do what's next, not what's easy." Those guys stapled insulation all day and then hosed themselves off in the parking lot, while fully clothed, to get the itchy fibers off them. Thousands have worshipped in a comfortable sanctuary because shadow Christians did that insulation dirty work.

Shadow Christians often do invisible tasks, the part of projects not seen by anyone except those doing it. We have already considered the four men who brought their disabled friend to Jesus (chapter 6). They were part of an early demo crew who took the roof off the building where Jesus was teaching. This was likely a thatch roof of some sort, meaning it wasn't a neat project. Sticks, clods, and dirt likely rained down on Jesus and his listeners as the roof was pulverized and pulled up. These guys did what had to be done to get their friend to Jesus.

Another example is the unnamed servants who helped when Jesus turned water into wine. Jesus prepared for the miracle by asking servants to fill up six stone water jars, each containing twenty to thirty gallons. They filled the jars "to the brim" (John 2:7). This meant someone had to move 120–180 gallons of water—not by turning on a hose but by hauling it in smaller containers from a well or a stream. Since a gallon of water

> **Shadow Christians often do invisible tasks, the part of projects not seen by anyone except those doing it.**

weighs about eight pounds, these anonymous servants moved about a thousand pounds of water to fill up those six water jars. Jesus then performed an amazing miracle, changing the water into wine. The servants did the grunt work, getting everything ready for the miracle to be performed. Jesus could have miraculously filled the jugs with wine without water being provided first. Instead, he asked unnamed servants to do their part in setting the stage for his supernatural activity.

Some people set the stage for others who lead in more public ways or complete more visible aspects of ministry projects. Shadow Christians are content to do their part, even when their work is later covered up or added to by others. They understand their role is preparatory, doing the unseen work to put everything in place for spotlight Christians to shine. Shadow Christians do what's next on the chore list, not what will be noticed by everyone when the project is finished.

Cleanup Crews

Jesus was facing a large hungry crowd of about five thousand men (plus women and children) with few apparent resources to meet their physical needs (Luke 9:10–17). The twelve disciples became concerned about feeding the multitude and encouraged Jesus to send them on their way. Instead, he had everyone sit in groups of fifty and fed all of them with five loaves and two fish. The end of the story seems so routine, "Everyone ate and was filled. They picked up twelve baskets of leftover pieces" (Luke 9:17). But who picked up the leftovers? Who found the baskets, sorted out the edibles, and set them aside for future use? Who was on the cleanup crew?

Some shadow Christians linger when a major event is over, sending leaders and other participants home with a casual, "We've got this." They anticipate and take on the thankless work required to finish almost any project.

A few years ago, our seminary moved our library from one location to another. My concern was the big picture—getting a reputable company, negotiating a reasonable price, making sure the new facility was ready, supervising the arrival of the shipments, and seeing the books go back on the shelves. Once all that was done, it seemed like the project was complete. Then, one day, I happened by the library and saw a worker going slowly down the stacks looking at every book. She was checking to be sure every book had been properly reshelved, in the right order, so students could find the books as coded in our computer systems. There were about 150,000 books! This shadow Christian was doing the final cleanup on the project to ensure the library was a useful tool, not a source of frustration, to future users. Shadow Christians push through to finish a job, including the cleanup details others often overlook.

Choosing a Dirty Job

For some believers, choosing a dirty job is more than an act of service. It becomes an intentional means to developing humility. The Bible advises, "Humble yourselves before the Lord, and he will exalt you" (James 4:10). When a person chooses self-abasement as an act of devotion with no expectation of reward, God lifts them up in due time.

Several years ago, a young man was promoted rapidly and became the general manager of a large department store. He was also a rising leader in his church. One Sunday, he was convicted about his pride in his accomplishments. He told the pastor, "I need to do something to remind myself where I came from and knock some of this pride out of me. If you have a dirty job at the church sometime soon, let me know, but don't tell anyone. I'd like to do it."

Two days later, the church had a major sewer backup in a main restroom. How quickly God answers some prayers! The sludge was several inches deep and had spread into the hallway and surrounding classrooms before it was found. When the pastor saw the mess, he thought, *Well, I wonder if he means it?* He called the young executive and told him what had happened. The man showed up a few minutes later—straight from work in a suit and tie—to start the cleanup. No one ever knew who handled that dirty job except the manager, the pastor, and me. I stopped by the church building to pick something up that day, saw the mess, offered to help, was turned down, and wondered why—given the scope (and smell) of the problem. The pastor briefed me on the situation and sent me on my way. A prideful man chose to do a dirty job to humble himself, trusting God to shape his character through the process.

Shadow Christians do the dirty work. They take the tough jobs that aren't even on the org chart. They prepare and serve meals, patrol parking lots, demolish old buildings, and clean up after parties. They sometimes volunteer for a dirty job to humble themselves, to practice self-abasement as a means of spiritual formation. Shadow Christians are willing to get down and dirty for ministry to be done effectively. They make sure whatever needs to be done gets done.

When you do the dirty work, you humble yourself and experience God's favor.

Group Discussion

1. What are some of the dirty jobs required for effective ministry in your church? Who does them? Do you do your part? If not, why not?

2. Why is hospitality important in ministry communities? Discuss with your group ways you can improve the hospitality it experiences and shows others.

3. Does your church provide any protective services? If so, how can you assist with this effort? Discuss ways your group can be involved in this ministry area.

4. Have you ever been on a mission trip or project with a "do the next thing" group mentality? If so, how did that impact what happened? Discuss with your group the possibility of doing a mission project together.

5. Read Luke 7:36–50. What can you learn from this woman's example? What positive results, besides her salvation experience, resulted from her service? Discuss the positive impact of doing dirty jobs with your group.

6. Read James 4:10 and 1 Peter 5:6. What does it mean to "humble yourself"? What will you do to obey this command?

7. Is there any task in your church you consider yourself too good to do or you consider beneath you? If so, why? Volunteer to do that job this week.

8. Discuss with your group the challenges faced by top-level leaders in your church—elders, deacons, or other leadership roles. Pray with your small group for the volunteer leaders in your church.

CHAPTER 9

WE LEAD CHURCHES

In the last two chapters, we celebrated believers filling out organizational charts and doing the dirty work not even included on the charts. These shadow Christians make a significant impact, particularly as volunteers in their churches. They may work in obscure service roles or as leaders for specific areas like women's ministry or building maintenance. Their sense of calling is often profound. These shadow Christians believe what they do matters to the overall success of their church fulfilling its mission. They are personally invested in their tasks and stay with them tenaciously. Without these brothers and sisters, churches would have limited functional ministry. They are the hands and feet of Jesus extended to and through their communities.

There's another group of volunteer church leaders, however, that oversees all of these shadow Christians—plus paid ministerial staff in many instances. While they are called different things in different churches or denominational traditions, the most common titles are elder and deacon. Considered collectively, these leaders are sometimes called a board or council or body. Some churches use contemporary language like leadership team or administrative team to describe their function. Whatever the title or job description determined by their church, they are a small band of highly committed volunteers who provide the spiritual, doctrinal, financial, and practical oversight of everything a church does.

Because their role entails local visibility and prominence, many assume these are spotlight Christians. But they aren't usually well-known outside their church context, and most of their work goes on behind-the-scenes. These shadow Christians are vital. Without them, particularly during rocky times, many churches would come unraveled. They are the leadership bedrock upon which long-lasting ministry rests, the glue that holds a church together through turbulent times.

Shadow Christians lead churches.

Church Leaders Emerge

The development of the early church, including the emergence of leaders like elders and deacons, is described in the book of Acts. The role of elders developed as the church was established in more and more places, recognizing the leaders needed to sustain the movement. The role originated in the Jerusalem church, although there's no clear record of how or when it happened.

The first mention of the elders in the Jerusalem church refers to them being entrusted with managing money to meet practical needs (Acts 11:30). About ten years after that church started at Pentecost (Acts 2), another church was launched at Antioch (Acts 11:19–24; see also chapter 10 in this book). Agabus, a visiting preacher from Jerusalem, asked the Antioch Christians for a famine relief offering to feed starving believers in Jerusalem (Acts 11:27–29). They gave an offering by "sending it to the elders [in Jerusalem] by means of Barnabas and Saul" (Acts 11:30). The first mention of New Testament church elders was as recipients and stewards of a disaster relief offering.

Although they cooperated in this offering, the Jerusalem and Antioch churches had different perspectives on an important doctrinal issue: the relationship of circumcision to salvation. That seems like an odd debate today! Circumcision was the historic symbol of God's covenant with Israel. Many Israelites wanted Gentiles to share this heritage by first being circumcised as part of becoming Christians. The broader question, which is relevant still today, was this: Does salvation depend on any human action, or is it entirely by God's grace through faith? The debate over this issue was contentious and resulted in tension among early believers.

When the Antioch church started (the first church among the Gentiles), many Jerusalem leaders opposed what was happening (because Gentiles were converting without being circumcised). They sent Barnabas to check out what was happening (Acts 11:22–23). He arrived as an inquisitor, not the encourager he was later famous for being. His task was to sort out the legitimacy of the Antioch movement. He faced two options: validate their conversion by grace through faith alone and entrance into the Christian community apart from circumcision or discredit their church entirely. Despite his reputation and deft handling of the problem (affirming the new believers in Antioch), the conflict persisted and resulted in a major showdown between the leaders of these two churches. It was a tense time as these groups later engaged "in serious argument and debate" (Acts 15:2).

The Antioch church ultimately sent a delegation to meet with the Jerusalem elders to resolve this issue (Acts 15:1–6). The stakes were high. The doctrine of salvation was on the line. Did conversion require circumcision or not? Is salvation really by grace through faith alone?

When the final decision was reached, the leaders from both churches affirmed salvation by grace through faith alone (Acts 15:22–23). The conclusion was well received in a larger context because it came from and included the elders who had met together in Jerusalem (Acts 16:4). These first elders were instrumental in settling doctrinal differences and reconciling relational tension between two churches. These events establish a precedent for some of the responsibilities of elders (and similar leaders) today.

As Paul and Barnabas started other churches, "when they had appointed elders for them in every church and prayed with fasting, they committed them to the Lord in whom they had believed" (Acts 14:23). These elders emerged relatively quickly, coming from among the converts who matured rapidly and assumed leadership roles. This is another important precedent and pattern. Church elders are usually homegrown leaders. They emerge from communities as a result of effective evangelism and discipleship strategies that produce church leaders.

One good example of this pattern was in Ephesus. Paul was instrumental in forming the church there (Acts 18:19–20; 19:1–41). Later, as he was about to depart from them, he summoned their elders and delivered a moving farewell message (Acts 20:17–35). In this speech, he charged the elders to "be on guard for yourselves and for all the flock of which the Holy Spirit has appointed you as overseers, to shepherd the church of God, which he purchased with his own blood. I know that after my departure savage wolves will come in among you, not sparing the flock. Men will rise up even from your own number and distort the truth to lure the disciples into following them" (Acts 20:28–30). Paul further challenged them to follow his example of working "with my own hands to support myself and those who are with me" and to "help the weak by laboring like this" (Acts 20:34–35). The profound bond between Paul and the Ephesian elders was shown by how their last encounter ended. Paul "knelt down and prayed with all of them. There were many tears shed by everyone. They embraced Paul and kissed him, grieving most of all over his statement that they would never see his face again. And they accompanied him to the ship" (Acts 20:36–38).

From this short summary of the emergence of these leaders, several aspects of church eldership can be seen. Elders emerge from communities as a result of evangelism, disciple making, and leadership development. They have wide-ranging responsibilities from managing relief offerings to assuring doctrinal integrity to solving fellowship problems between church members. Elders are examples of personal responsibility and generosity, usually providing their own financial support as volunteer leaders. They bond together in shared sacrifices for their church's mission and love for one another and the church they lead. They aren't detached managers but passionate Christians who put their lives on the line for the good of the church they serve and the advancement of God's kingdom.

The other significant leadership role in the early church was deacon. That title isn't specifically mentioned in Acts. Some interpret the selection of ministry workers in Jerusalem (seven named men) as a precursor to deacons (Acts 6:1–7). Making this connection, given the way deacons are later described (1 Tim. 3:8–13), is permissible and perhaps likely (but not definitive). The other possible deacon reference in Acts is to Phoebe, elsewhere called a "servant of the church" in some translations and a "deaconess" in others (Rom. 16:1). This description may be a reference to her reputation for service or to a more formal role.

The qualifications for both elders and deacons aren't described in detail until about thirty years after the church started at Pentecost (1 Tim. 3:1–13; Titus 1:5–9). These passages provide a fuller description of those roles, how they had developed over time, and how important they had become to the early church. They also underscore how essential elders and deacons are for church leadership today.

No Names Mentioned

One noticeable absence from every reference to elders and deacons in the Bible is their names. While elders are prominent and deacons are hinted at in Acts, there isn't one person called "Elder Tom" or "Deacon Bob" who had their name recorded. While seven men and one woman are named in Acts and associated with deacon-like functions, none are definitively named and/or titled as deacons.

Even though Paul included the names of many ministry partners in his letters, he never wrote about an elder or deacon by name. That's a striking omission for people so vital to the development of the early church. The key leaders in the emerging churches in the New Testament were shadow Christians. They served in prominent roles and provided courageous leadership in anonymity. Their biblical example established the standard by which these leaders are measured and the pattern by which they serve today.

> **The key leaders in the emerging churches in the New Testament were shadow Christians.**

Elders and deacons take on the difficult tasks of handling church conflicts, decisions, and struggles without remuneration or public accolades. They serve after hours, when their secular workday is done, taking on thorny problems related to all aspects of church life. These shadow Christians tirelessly provide the overarching leadership churches need to accomplish their mission. This usually includes working closely with (and often supervising) vocational ministers, which requires additional wisdom and courage. Significant shadow leaders, elders and deacons are the mainstays of effective church leadership.

Glue Guys

Coaches call some players glue guys. These are players who hold a team together. They are seldom the best athletes or the most prominent players. More often, they make the block so the star can score a touchdown or set the screen so the star can make the game-winning shot. Glue guys smooth out team conflicts and make sure everyone feels like they belong to the group. They organize team dinners, take a fellow player aside who needs correction or encouragement, and speak a quiet word to their coach when he needs to address an unseen problem. Glue guys don't get their name on the marquee and aren't interviewed on the postgame show. They work in the shadows.

Elders and deacons are glue guys who hold a church together. They fulfill important roles many people hardly notice until no one does them. Then *everyone* notices because of the damage done to the church's ministry or reputation. The negative results of a leadership vacuum illustrate how important elders and deacons really are. Here are three ways these shadow leaders sustain churches. This isn't all they do, but these leadership adhesives help hold a church together.

Permanent Leadership

Elders and deacons usually emerge from within their church in contrast to pastors who often come from the outside. They are plumbers, teachers, business owners, and retirees who have deep roots in their community. They are a stabilizing force in light of three particular realities. First, elders and deacons provide leadership continuity given the short-term pastoral tenures in many American churches. Second, they round out the leadership team in large numbers of churches that have a bivocational or part-time pastor. Third, elders and deacons provide continuity during pastoral transition whether cleaning up the damage of a failed pastorate or paving the way for a new person during a more positive changeover. Consistent, embedded, community-committed leaders provide the permanent leadership churches need.

Protective Leadership

Elders and/or deacons, depending on how those roles are defined by a church, are responsible for a church's doctrinal integrity. Paul included this charge to the Ephesian elders (Acts 20:28–31) and made it part of his qualification lists (1 Tim. 3:1–13; Titus 1:5–9). Church leaders must be on guard against external and internal threats to theological convictions. They do this by ensuring their church's doctrinal statement is thoroughly biblical, clearly written, and communicated to every person. They also do it by monitoring what is taught by their church—in both preaching and teaching settings, for all ages and life stages—to make sure it aligns with their doctrinal statement. Confronting these issues is some of the most difficult work they do. It involves careful study, frank dialogue, courageous decision making, and handling the painful backlash when a popular communicator is removed from his or her teaching position.

Personal Example

Elders and deacons provide a personal standard of Christian commitment and behavior others can emulate. Paul challenged the Ephesian elders to be examples of industry and generosity (Acts 20:32–35). His lists of qualifications for both elders and deacons focus more on character strength, relational skills, and family health than ministry abilities (1 Tim. 3:1–13; Titus 1:5–9). These church leaders are thermostats, not thermometers. They set the spiritual temperature and behavioral standards, giving church members an example to follow. Elders and deacons are Christian role models. They aren't perfect, but they are steady models of spiritual growth, personal deportment, family commitment, and ministry engagement. They demonstrate what it means to live by convictions in these important areas.

Quiet Quality

Elders and deacons are a special brand of shadow Christians. They take on the challenge of church leadership, committing themselves to a lifetime of unseen service. They love God and his church. They also love pastors and want them to succeed. For every "idiot elder" or "crazy deacon" story, there are hundreds of these leaders whose spiritual devotion and steady service humble and inspire those who have worked with them.

Andy is one example. He owned a home-decorating business and served his church as a deacon. He also taught an adult Sunday school class, sang in the choir, and went out of his way to help me (as a college student) learn how to make ministerial visits with people in their homes.

One night was typical. After a worship service he asked me to go with him to see someone. During the drive, he said, "I've been talking to this man about the Lord. I think he is becoming more open to the gospel. I want to try to share it with him tonight. You pray for me as I talk to him."

We arrived at a ramshackle trailer house in a rough part of town. I wondered how a successful businessman even knew anyone in that neighborhood. We went into the trailer, pushed the cats off the couch, and found a place to sit. Before long Andy was sharing the gospel with a one-legged, homebound man in a tattered work shirt. Before we left that night, he professed faith in Jesus. Andy later arranged for him to get baptized and become part of our church.

This good deacon did this kind of work, consistently and without notoriety, for years. If he were looking over my shoulder right now, he would say, "Jeff, don't write that. I never did that much. Just tried to serve the Lord, help the pastor, and support the church." But since he's in heaven, he's not here to stop me from moving his story from backstage to center stage.

Another group of deacons served with me in my first pastorate. At first, I thought they were hopeless impediments to my supposedly visionary leadership. At twenty-four years old, I was sure I was the fire-hot pastor they needed to lead their church to greatness. When things didn't go as I planned and chaos ensued, they stood with me and helped me pick up the pieces of the mess I had made. Once we all got on the same page—or rather, once I learned enough to start being a more effective pastor, the church surged forward.

After a few years, I asked them for time off to work on a doctoral degree. I proposed a plan that involved using vacation time and additional unpaid leave to earn the degree. They listened to my request and told me they would consider it. The chairman said, "We'll talk this over, and I'll come by your office tomorrow and let you know what we decide." The next day he told me, "We want you to do the program. Forget using your vacation or unpaid leave. You need to take that time for your family. We are going to ask the church to give you paid time off. And we checked with your school on how much this is going to cost. We're going to pay for your doctorate."

When I asked why they were doing this, he replied, "We believe in you and your future. We want to be part of it." Among those men, there was only one college graduate. That's part of what made their sacrifice for my education so amazing. One of them later told me, after I had left to plant a church and then became a denominational executive, "We knew you would someday leave our church and God would use your leadership gifts in a larger place. We knew it was part of our job to get you ready." Those shadow Christians, unknown outside a Midwestern church, propelled me forward to influence tens of thousands of people through leading, speaking, teaching, and writing. It's time for their story to come out of the shadows as well.

These are examples of how volunteer church leaders impact their church, their community, and the kingdom of God. Almost every well-known Christian leader or prominent pastor can point to men and women who have served with them (and served them) as elders, deacons, or in similar roles. Sure, there are occasional lapses among these leaders, even some horror stories. But those are novellas compared to the volumes recording how elders and deacons have served and sustained their churches through the centuries.

Show Some Love

If you serve in the shadows as an elder or deacon (or comparable leadership role), thank you! You don't expect accolades, but accept a few nonetheless. You are making a significant contribution to God's kingdom. You are part of the permanent leadership base in your church, the footings that hold firm in every storm. Part of your job is to protect your church from doctrinal error, financial mismanagement, relational conflict, and missional drift. Be relentless, measured, and determined in fulfilling those duties. You are also an example of what it means to be a Christian. Your character qualities, relational skills, and family dynamics are models for others. That's a heavy burden but a good one God will help you bear. You are influencing others by your quiet devotion and consistent choices.

You are also a vital support to your pastor or pastoral team. Leading a church is hard work. It's spiritually taxing, emotionally draining, and relationally demanding. Your pastor needs partners who support him when he struggles, tell him the truth when he is wrong, stand with him when he is right, and defend him when he is attacked or criticized. Good elders and deacons have a backbone! They stand up and do what's right, even when it's hard or unpopular.

If you aren't serving in one of these roles, you likely know someone who is. Show them some love. Let them know you appreciate the work they do. Send a thank-you note. Drop them an encouraging email. Stop them after church and say, "Thank you for your leadership." Some elders and deacons have served for years, even decades. Find a way to honor their longevity. Don't wait until their memorial service to express appreciation for them. They deserve better, and we must do more in showing love to them.

Pray for your elders, deacons, and other church leaders. Ask God to give them wisdom, stamina, and spiritual insight. Pray for them to have discernment and vision. Pray against devilish division among leaders. Confront faultfinders who gossip or criticize church leaders or their families. Challenge misinformation or presumptions people have about them. Insist recalcitrant members talk directly to church leaders rather than being their sounding board and allowing their attacks to go unchecked.

Finally, train future elders and deacons. These leaders will emerge in your church if you have an intentional strategy for producing the next generation of people for these roles. Do all you can to make sure your church has the leadership base it needs for sustained vitality. Elders and deacons are significant shadow Christians who make a vital difference in church leadership today.

Thank God for shadow Christians who take on church leadership roles.

Group Discussion

1. Review the section above about the origin of elders and deacons in Acts. What are some of the key functions of these leaders? Why were their names omitted from the stories about them? Discuss your ideas with your group.

2. Read 1 Timothy 3:1–13 and Titus 1:5–9. What are the key qualities and requirements of church leaders? Why are character and relationships emphasized more than skills in these lists?

3. What are the three "leadership adhesives" mentioned in this chapter? Discuss with your group how permanent leadership, protective leadership, and personal example are expressed by the leaders in your church.

4. Share a story with your group of the positive impact an elder or deacon has had in your life. Celebrate the stories others share.

5. What kinds of difficult situations do elders and deacons handle behind the scenes? Discuss with your group how to be supportive when one of these situations occurs in your church.

6. What are some ways you can show appreciation for elders and deacons? Choose one way and do it this week. In your group, pray for the elders and deacons of your

church. Ask God to raise up future leaders within your church.

7. Shadow Christians serve at all levels on the org chart—as workers, mid-level leaders, and senior leaders. Have you found your place to serve? Are you serving well? Pray with your group for the grace to serve faithfully.

8. Shadow Christians are important in expanding God's kingdom and beyond their church. As you prepare to read the next chapter, discuss with your group some ways you can be involved in kingdom ministries beyond your church.

CHAPTER 10

WE START CHURCHES AND MINISTRIES

Most new movements begin as the dream of a person or group of people who sacrifice time, energy, and money to bring them to reality. New churches are birthed this way. We experienced this when our family moved cross-country to start a new church near Portland, Oregon. Now, about thirty years later, we are involved in launching another new church near our home in California. Starting new things seems to be in our family's DNA. Both of my sons have started companies, and my daughter is married to a church-planting pastor! We have lived the joys and pains of starting things, from a new church when our three children were preschoolers to new entities as adults. Whether it's a company, church, or ministry, everything has a beginning.

Because mature companies and ministries often have prominent leaders, it's easy to mistakenly conclude they also had superstar founders. In most instances that's not the case. Some founders are remarkable people who grow in stature as their entity grows, like Rick Warren who started Saddleback Church and became a global leader. Jeff Bezos, Amazon founder and one of the richest men in the world, was once an unknown dreamer with an unproven business plan for online retailing. People like Warren and Bezos are exceptions. Most organizations are started by groundbreakers whose identity is largely forgotten over time, not superstars who stay on the stage for a generation (keep reading for some humorous examples of how this happened to me).

Most companies, churches, and ministries weren't started by their current leaders. Most founders don't become household names. Their individual stories are often lost in history or subsumed in organizational success. But without those entrepreneurs, today's thriving organizations wouldn't be possible. Without unnamed founders who turned dreams into reality, whether in ministry or business, nothing consequential could have later been built.

God specializes in choosing obscure people like Gideon (Judg. 6:15) or David (1 Sam. 16:11) to launch new initiatives or to lead in new directions. While people like these were named, the Bible also tells the stories of unnamed people who started new movements. God used faithful, unknown, and unnamed people to fulfill big dreams. He still inspires visionaries to pursue the future with reckless abandon, infusing them with an urgency to innovate, to do something new. When an imaginative leader or a group of believers is willing to do that, new churches and ministries are born. Superstars are appreciated but not necessary for God to start something new. All he needs are followers committed to innovating the future with him.

Shadow Christians start new churches and ministries.

The Genesis Point

The idea for this book originated in a study of some anonymous church planters. The Bible tells their story this way: "Now those who had been scattered as a result of the persecution that started because of Stephen made their way as far as Phoenicia, Cyprus, and Antioch, speaking the word to no one except Jews. But there were some of them, men from Cyprus and Cyrene, who came to Antioch and began speaking to the Greeks also, proclaiming the good news about the Lord Jesus. The Lord's hand was with them, and a large number who believed turned to the Lord" (Acts 11:19–21). That's all the background information we have on the men who started the most significant church in the New Testament era and perhaps in world history. Notice, no names mentioned.

Antioch was significant because it was a church of firsts, initiated by and resulting from entrepreneurial founders. The first and perhaps most striking innovation at Antioch was the establishment of the church itself. In the early years of the Christian movement, the gospel was retained by the Jewish community, and the church largely remained in Jerusalem. Exceptions were rare and usually happened after persecution forced Jerusalem-based believers to flee for their lives (for example, Acts 8:1). Early exceptions include Philip's ministry in Samaria (Acts 8:4–13) and later with the Ethiopian eunuch (Acts 8:26–39). Another exception was Peter's travels, resulting in his vision of the edible animals preparing him for his visit to Cornelius (Acts 10:1–48). These incidents were precursors to the expansion of the gospel among Gentiles. They stand out as exceptions to the prevailing practice of the early church, which was witnessing the gospel to Jews. Stephen's persecution, which prompted the scattering of men like Philip (Acts 8:1–4) and Peter (Acts 9:32–10:48), was also the impetus for others to travel as far as Antioch (Acts 11:19).

These unnamed men made their way as far as "Phoenicia, Cyprus, and Antioch, speaking the word to no one except Jews" (Acts 11:19). So far, despite the command of Jesus (Acts 1:8) and examples of Philip and Peter (the Antioch church planters may or may not have been aware of their work), the early church had remained a Jewish-focused, Jerusalem-centered movement. That was all about to change.

While other itinerant preachers had labored among Jews, "there were some of them, men from Cyprus and Cyrene, who came to Antioch and began speaking to the Greeks also, proclaiming the good news about the Lord Jesus" (Acts 11:20). These anonymous men—never named in the Bible, their identities lost in church history—broke the mold and began preaching the gospel in a Gentile community. While that seems like standard operating procedure today, at the time it was a courageous act by men who risked their lives to advance the gospel. Generations of Jewish tradition and years of early Christian practice mandated these brave men be circumspect with the gospel. Yet they cast aside all restraint, preached the gospel to Gentiles, "and a large number who believed turned to the Lord" (Acts 11:21).

After a few years had passed, another innovation at Antioch was launching the first intentional missionary movement. This major breakthrough was the natural result of the epoch-shaping actions that started the church in the first place. During a worship service, the Holy Spirit told church members to send Barnabas and Paul to share the gospel and start new churches in other cities (Acts 13:1–3). The tone of the story suggests the church responded quickly to those directions, and "after they had fasted, prayed, and laid hands on them, they sent them off" (Acts 13:3). It's interesting to note the missionary call came to and through unnamed church members, not by way of the prominent leaders who actually became the missionaries. Even in this story, which featured two spotlight leaders (Barnabas and Paul), God used shadow

Christians to launch the first intentional missionary movement.

This first mission trip resulted in converts and new churches in places like Cyprus, Pisidian Antioch, Iconium, Lystra, and Derbe (Acts 13:4–14:28). The missionary team eventually returned to Antioch. After they "gathered the church together, they reported everything God had done with them and that he had opened the door of faith to the Gentiles. And they spent a considerable time with the disciples" (Acts 14:27–28). The Antioch church's continued support, interest, and accountability for the missionary team is shown both in their response to the trip-reporting service and in their later sending the team on additional trips.

God used shadow Christians to launch the first intentional missionary movement.

The Antioch church planters are towering heroes of our faith, particularly if you are a Gentile believer. Without their courageous willingness to innovate—preaching the gospel in a way it had never been preached, to a people who had never heard it, in a city where it had never been shared—you would likely not be a Christian today. Because of these men, the gospel finally broke the shackles of Jewish religious tradition and became good news for all people everywhere, as God had always intended. Paul and Barnabas were launched from Antioch, not just to the Mediterranean world but to create a movement extending to your Gentile church today. Those unnamed men from Cyprus and Cyrene, if you are a Gentile believer, are your spiritual forefathers.

Studying the example of these men motivated me to continue their legacy and plant a church. Being the founding pastor of a new church was a seminal privilege. God used me as the up-front leader. But the real heroes were the shadow Christians who built the church into the ministry powerhouse it has become. They were full partners on the church planting team. Their commitment and sacrifice were significant factors in launching the church and growing it to strength over the years. And, as in Antioch, they have continued the movement by starting other churches in their area and sending missionary teams around the world. Let's bring some of their stories out of the shadows to inspire you to do the same.

Two Couples with a Dream

Rusty and Sheila and Bill and Alice had a burden and a dream for a new church in Gresham, Oregon. They were commuting a significant distance to their respective churches but lived in the same suburb, which had limited church options. Their dream was a vibrant church for their community. They met and talked and prayed, then shared their idea with a denominational leader who facilitated church planting. After a few months that leader spoke at a conference I attended. We had lunch together, I shared my initial thoughts about planting a church somewhere in the Western United States, and he told me about the two couples who were praying for a church planter to come to their community. After a process of discovery and consideration, our family decided to move to Oregon and plant a new church.

While we were in the decision-making process, two other couples—Glenn and Inez and Maynard and Bev—decided to help start the church. Before we moved, some other people (believers and unbelievers) heard about the new church and indicated interest in helping get it started. Soon after we arrived in Oregon, there were about twenty adults considering becoming part of the new church along with a slew of teenagers and kids. We later called the first two couples the "core four" in our church planting history.

In the early years, many other people joined the church, most as new followers of Jesus. Some of their shadow stories are the reasons the church is so strong today. Their anonymous sacrifice, commitment, and perseverance made the difference.

Stepping Out of the Shadows

The shadow Christians who planted the church didn't do it to make a name for themselves—much less have their stories included in a book. Who were these remarkable people? Rusty was an accountant; Sheila, a homemaker. Alice was a teacher and Bill an educational administrator. Bev worked in a communications department. Maynard drove a truck. Glenn and Inez were retired but young enough in heart to, in their words, "help start a church for young families." This small group did it all to start the church—passed out flyers, invited their friends, set up in a public school each week, provided childcare, ran the sound system, led the youth group (just a few teenagers the first year), and gave their money. They worked hard with little recognition and no guarantee a new church would actually survive in the unchurched Pacific Northwest.

Besides the core four, others came along to help. Steve was the first convert and became the audio guy. Kathy and Cathy both joined the worship team. David played the bass and Shirley the piano. Gary prepared the Sunday refreshments. Bob and Buff taught a class. Roberta hosted events at her house. Elmer and Quilla established a missions program. Brian was a greeter. Bernie kept the books and paid the bills. Dale ran the projector in the worship service. Wayne led the Sunday worship, and Nancy hosted the weeknight rehearsals at her house. Cindy organized fellowships. Robin taught children. Sue Ann and Ann did whatever anyone else didn't do. Joe organized the whole thing.

These shadow Christians were the impetus for what has become a healthy church with a global ministry footprint. While the church's pastoral leaders have been invited to speak in conferences, serve on boards, and provide denominational leadership, the shadow Christians did the hard work to build a great church. Some of them are now in heaven, some have followed job and life changes to new communities, and others are still actively serving in the same church as senior adults. Thirty years goes by fast! As the founding pastor of this church, my memories of the work done by these friends are humbling and gratifying. God rallied them around my public leadership to do the behind-the-scenes tasks of building a healthy church.

Then, to everyone's surprise, God called me to leave the pastorate of the church of my dreams but to remain in the church. My role went from visible leader to supportive member overnight. It was my turn to be a shadow Christian, at least at my home church. The Antioch church planters had inspired me. Now I was following their example into anonymity. Just as their names were lost in history, mine was soon to be forgotten at our church—only faster and more humorously than anyone imagined.

Forgotten, Three Times

Spotlight leaders (even ministry founders) are easily forgotten when they drift into the shadows. When I resigned from being the founding pastor and took a denominational position (which required Sunday travel to other churches), my wife continued to serve as our church's preschool director. About a year after I had left, she accidentally overheard a woman tell a friend, "I love our church's preschool ministry. Ann does such a great job with this program. But we need to pray for her husband. He never comes to church. We need to pray for him to be saved." After my wife stopped laughing, she stepped in the hall and said, "Ladies, I'm sorry I overheard your conversation, but just one clarification." She told them about my ministry position and that I had been the founding pastor of the church. They had no idea. Gone for a year and completely unknown to newer members!

Sometime later, after we moved from the area, we returned and visited the church on a Sunday morning. During the worship service there was a meet-and-greet time. A member shook my hand and asked, "Is this your first time here? We're glad you came and hope you'll come again." I just smiled and said, "Thank you. We have been here before and we'll be back." It was funny the first time and even funnier when the same thing happened with different greeters the next two times we visited the church. Again, gone and quickly forgotten!

But the best story happened fifteen years after we moved away. We hosted a Gateway Seminary board meeting in Oregon and took some trustees to the church for Sunday worship. As part of the service, a younger associate pastor extended a welcome to all guests. He singled out our group and said, "We would like to welcome

Jeff Iorg and the trustees from Gateway Seminary to our service. Dr. Iorg was once on the staff of our church—or something." It was an awesome moment! I had done something, but the young brother (who had not been born when the church started) couldn't remember what it was. The founding pastor just wasn't on his radar.

You might think, *That's not right! They should have remembered you and honored you.* No! It's much better the church has continued to grow, reach more people, develop a new generation of leaders, and live in the present, not the past. It's much better longtime members are the minority and the church is perpetually new because it's reaching more people. These stories are positive examples of healthy forgetfulness.

Shadow Christians celebrate when the spotlight shines on others, in the present, who enjoy the fruit of their past labors. Shadow Christians don't pout and say, "What about me?" They celebrate their role in launching a church, a ministry, a company, or an organization. They revel in how it's accomplishing the mission for which it was started, not how it glorifies their past contribution. Their legacy is present success, not past memories. Carrying on the mission that inspired the initial vision is the best way to honor past leaders as well as

> **Shadow Christians celebrate when the spotlight shines on others.**

the contribution of shadow Christians who made fulfilling it possible.

Be a Kick-Starter

The best time to plant a shade tree was ten years ago. The next best time is today. The best time to have started a ministry to meet present needs was ten years ago. If someone had done so, it would likely be flourishing by now. But since that didn't happen, the next best time to start a new church or ministry in your community is now. While a visible leader may take the point, it will take a team of shadow Christians to make it happen. You may not be an entrepreneurial leader, but you can certainly be on the team.

You can help start a new church. One of the most pressing needs for church planters is dependable believers who will round out a church starting team. Church planters need people to set up equipment, manage the website, operate worship technology, manage money, develop programs for children and teenagers, start a prayer ministry, organize and execute outreach projects, and—most of all—share the gospel in their community (see chapter 6). Church planters and new churches also need money, which means they need gainfully employed members who give tithes and offerings (see chapter 11). The strength of a church plant isn't solely determined by the pastor's speaking abilities or visionary leadership.

It's also determined by the people who give time, energy, expertise, and money to get the job done.

You can also help start a new ministry in your church or community. Starting something new usually begins with discovering a pressing need no one is meeting. God has a way of bringing a need to the awareness of people who will become concerned about the problem. New ministries often start at the intersection of need and passion. Shadow Christians don't say, "*Someone* should do something about that." They think, *What can we do about this?* They understand that doing something, even a small thing, is better than whining about unmet needs. They also realize the importance of doing their part, trusting God to multiply their efforts and motivating others to get involved.

Willing to Be Forgotten

Once you have helped start a church or ministry, even if you are there long enough for it to reach maturity (and for you to reach "maturity" as well), it will someday be time to turn it over to others. Do so intentionally and graciously. Don't cling to the past or hold onto a ministry because it's comfortable, gives you satisfaction, or affirms your identity. Recognize when it's time to fade into the shadows or disappear from the stage altogether. Be willing to be forgotten, content the movement you helped start will keep going. Celebrate the mission being perpetually accomplished as your living legacy instead of memorializing your role in starting or sustaining the organization.

The Antioch church planters started a church that put the missionary movement among Gentiles in motion. Their work has cascaded through more than twenty centuries. Their impact is seen in every non-Jewish Christian congregation in the world today. That's an amazing contribution to God's kingdom, yet no one knows their names. You can make a similar impact even when no one knows yours.

When I get to heaven, I want to meet those Antioch planters and thank them. They are ultimate missionary heroes—selfless, anonymous, and effective in making a multigenerational contribution to the advance of the gospel. Who started your church? Dig around in the historical records and see if you can learn anything about them. Celebrate those men and women as your spiritual foreparents and then pay it forward to the next generation.

You can make the same kind of impact, even from the shadows. Take the risk to join a church-planting team. Pair up with a few people and start a new ministry. Be a founding team member of an innovative enterprise in God's kingdom. Visionary leaders matter, but so do shadow Christians who make their dreams a reality.

You can help start new churches and ministries.

Group Discussion

1. Why do we focus more on current leaders than founding leaders in churches and ministry organizations? Why are many founders forgotten? How is this a positive development?

2. Read Acts 11:19–30 and 13:1–3. What were some of the innovations—things that happened for the first time—in Antioch? How could your church follow this model and become more effective? Discuss these ideas with your group.

3. Why are everyday people important team members for church planting? Ask someone in your group to share their experience with church planting.

4. Is someone starting a new church in your community? Are you willing to be on the team to do this? Why or why not? Discuss your concerns or hopes about church planting with your group.

5. Does someone need to start a new ministry in or through your church? What need would it meet? Are you willing to be on the team to do this? Discuss the possibilities with your group.

6. Do you have a story of being forgotten or overlooked? How did you feel when it happened? Why? Share this

experience with your group. Listen to the stories of others. Discuss with your group ways to get over any emotional pain from this experience.

7. Why is it hard for people to fade away from a ministry they have helped start or have invested in for many years? What are some spiritual motivations for exiting gracefully? Share an example of someone who has done this well with your group.

8. Besides starting new churches and ministries, another way shadow Christians expand God's kingdom is through giving. What reservations do you have about studying this subject? Pray with your group and ask God for insight into biblical generosity.

CHAPTER 11

WE FUND CHURCHES AND MINISTRIES

N o margin, no ministry" was the succinct way one leader summarized the importance of adequate funding for any church or Christian organization. His meaning is clear. Every ministry has to take in one more dollar than it spends to survive.

It's a hard reality, not a secular concession, that ministry leadership includes gathering, managing, and effectively using financial resources.

Some leaders overspiritualize financial issues, especially where the money comes from to fund ministry. Some naively assume God will take care of their needs without them working out a detailed plan. They equate frank financial discussions and hard-nosed planning with worldliness, giving too much attention to money concerns instead of trusting God. In their minds, too much planning discounts faith in God to provide.

Some ministry leaders believe other people are responsible to fund their work. They look to denominational sources or grants to pay their bills but don't want to be involved in raising money themselves.

Another problem is leaders confusing trusting God to provide with presuming on his provision. The former makes bold plans and moves ahead as God confirms his direction and timing by his provision. The latter creates financial obligations and assumes someone else will later make the payments on the debt they incur.

These flawed perspectives on ministry finance—fanciful bookkeeping, charitable resourcing, and debt financing—reflect an immature understanding of how God funds ministry.

All this leads to the critical question, How does God provide for the work he is doing in the world today? The short answer: through gifts from people. Some who read that sentence subconsciously add the word *rich* before *people*. That's an inaccurate insertion, as you will soon discover. Most of the money fueling ministry today comes from everyday people, not a few prosperous donors. Most of it comes from people like you.

Shadow Christians fund ministry.

God through People

Who provides ministry money? The short, spiritual, and correct answer: God provides. God is our Source and Sustainer, period. But while financial resources come from God, they almost always pass through someone's hands on the way to a church's bank account. Who are these donors? They are rank-and-file Christians who give relatively small amounts consistently, quietly, sacrificially—who make a significant impact when combined with the gifts of fellow believers. Most people who earn, gather, and give the money to fund churches and ministries do so out of obedience and gratitude to God, not to gain notoriety. You are likely numbered among these generous shadow Christians who enable ministry by your giving.

There are multiple stories in the Bible, both during Jesus' ministry and the developing years of the early church, that illustrate how unnamed people provided materials for the mission. On several occasions (including two in the last week of his life on Earth), Jesus directed his disciples to collect necessary resources. They did so with little fanfare and no mention of the donors' names.

Jesus told two of his disciples, "Go into the village ahead of you. As you enter it, you will find a colt tied there, on which no one has ever sat. Untie it and bring it. If anyone asks you, 'Why are you untying it?' say this: 'The Lord needs it'" (Luke 19:30–31). The disciples found the animal and, as might be expected, questions were raised. "As they were untying the colt, its owners said to them, 'Why are you untying the colt?' 'The Lord needs it,' they said" (Luke 19:33–34), "so they let them go" (Mark 11:6). The most famous colt in history was provided by an anonymous donor.

A few days later, it was time for the Passover, the most important Jewish religious holiday. The disciples asked Jesus where he planned to observe it. He told two of them, "Go into the city, and a man carrying a jar of water will meet you. Follow him. Wherever he enters, tell the owner of the house, 'The Teacher says, "Where is my guest room where I may eat the Passover with my disciples?"' He will show you a large room upstairs, furnished and ready. Make the preparations for us there" (Mark 14:13–15).

In both cases, disciples followed Jesus' directions and made the arrangements. Just as he foreknew and instructed, a colt and a furnished room were provided. Jesus identified specific people who would channel necessary provisions. Isn't it interesting that despite his capacity to know everything and predict the minute details in these stories, these two donors—colt owner and home owner—remain anonymous? Their gifts mattered more than their identity.

Two other well-known giving stories during Jesus' ministry also underscore the significance of small gifts given by unnamed donors. When a large crowd needed to be fed and a solution seemed impossible, Andrew said, "There's a boy here who has five barley loaves and two fish—but what are they for so many?" (John 6:9). This is one of the few stories told in all four Gospels, underscoring its significance. Besides John, however, no other writer includes the detail that a boy provided the loaves and fish. An unnamed boy, only mentioned once, was the means by which God provided. Jesus took this limited provision, blessed it, and fed five thousand people with enough leftovers to fill twelve baskets. One of the most consequential offerings in history was given by a child who was barely mentioned, much less named.

Jesus also used a small gift by another unnamed donor to teach important lessons about true generosity. Jesus was sitting across from the temple treasury watching people give their offerings. Rich people were making generous, showy donations. "Then a poor widow came and dropped in two tiny coins worth very little. Summoning his disciples, he said to them, 'Truly I tell you, this poor widow has put more into the treasury than all the others. For they all gave out of their surplus, but she out of her poverty has put in everything she had—all she had to live on'" (Mark 12:42–44). Jesus made it clear that sacrifice matters more than show; proportion matters more than amount.

> **Most shadow Christians aren't fat cats or high rollers. They are everyday believers.**

Shadow Christians are like the people in these biblical stories. They are farmers and homeowners, children with limited resources, and seniors living on fixed incomes. They give what they have: an animal from the herd, hospitality and a spare room, their lunch money, or part of their Social Security check. Most shadow Christians aren't fat cats or high rollers. They are everyday believers like you. They know all they have comes from God, and he expects them to be good stewards. They are channels of God's resources, not holding ponds behind dams erected by their selfishness or need to be noticed.

Church Channeled Giving

Most of the giving shadow Christians do today is to and through their churches. This is both a biblical pattern and practical necessity. The church is God's priority method for advancing his kingdom, including training people to disciple their money toward that end. While parachurch ministries have their place, in the long run their strength depends on the financial health of strong churches that train new stewards. Through churches the most effective work of evangelizing the lost, making disciples of new converts, and shaping disciples into leaders takes place. Local churches do the best job of meeting the needs of entire communities, not just the particular, specialized groups targeted by niche ministries. Parachurch organizations draw their resources, and thus their financial strength, from Christians who have been shaped into generous givers and given a passion for global ministry by their churches.

Church-focused giving is modeled by believers in Acts. One of the earliest examples happened at Antioch. The church started among Gentiles (with no background in biblical giving patterns) who soon learned the importance of giving (perhaps as a result of the teaching ministry, Acts 11:26). They gave the first recorded offerings for disaster relief and church planting. A preacher named Agabus, from Jerusalem, spoke to the Antioch church and "predicted by the Spirit that there would be a severe famine throughout the Roman world" (Acts 11:28). In response, "each of the disciples, according to his ability, determined to send relief to the brothers and sisters who lived in Judea" (Acts 11:29). There are several important lessons in the story of this first recorded offering received as part of a worship service in Acts.

The first Antioch offering was given by "each of the disciples." Participation was widespread and individualized; each disciple gave an offering (the church did not just "cut a check"). It was given by believers to alleviate hunger from a famine. Thus, the first offering was a relief offering to mitigate the effects of a natural disaster. It was given by members of a church (Antioch) to help members of another church (Jerusalem). Each person gave "according to his ability" (Acts 11:29). This is a significant detail in the story. The Gentiles who formed the Antioch church weren't steeped in Old Testament giving practices, particularly the concept of tithing (based on proportional giving). They had somehow learned that God's giving expectations are based on proportionality, not just amounts. "According to his ability" means the rich gave a lot and the poor gave a little. They each gave a proportion of what they had, not a fixed amount.

The most striking part of this offering story, however, is who gave the offering, and to whom it was given. By the time this offering happened, the Jerusalem church was nearly ten years old. As we saw in an earlier chapter, they had bottled up the gospel, making circumcision a requirement for conversion and inclusion in the Christian movement. There was enough tension about this issue that the Jerusalem church sent Barnabas to determine the Antioch church's legitimacy (Acts 11:22). This problem was so severe it later resulted in the first major meeting to resolve a doctrinal conflict: the Jerusalem Council (Acts 15:1–35). The Jerusalem church had resisted the gospel's advance among Gentiles, questioned the legitimacy of the conversions at Antioch, and insisted circumcision was essential to becoming a Christian. While this conflict was brewing (long before the resolution in Acts 15), they sent Agabus to Antioch to ask for an offering. And, amazingly, the Antioch church gave one! Feeding hungry people trumped doctrinal and relational tensions. Shadow Christians often understand this better than their leaders. Hurting people have to be helped, no matter their religious or political beliefs, no matter past racial or ethnic conflicts.

Later another worship service at Antioch was marked by generous giving. "As they were worshiping the Lord and fasting, the Holy Spirit said, 'Set apart for me Barnabas and Saul for the work to which I have called them.' Then after they had fasted, prayed, and laid hands on them, they sent them off" (Acts 13:2–3). Unnamed Antioch church members gathered for worship, sensed the Holy Spirit's direction, decided to send their best leaders as church planters, and provided the resources to support them in itinerate ministry. While the phrase "sent them off" doesn't specifically describe an offering, other passages support the conclusion churches like Antioch (and others) gave missionary offerings to support those they commissioned (for example, 2 Cor. 8:1–5). Shadow Christians send missionaries, with the necessary financial support, to expand God's kingdom. They even sacrifice by sending their best leaders so the gospel can be shared effectively in new places.

The Myth of Big Donors

Because large gifts attract attention, many people mistakenly believe rich donors are the key to funding churches and ministries. They aren't. The foundation of ministry finance is the vast number of everyday people who give relatively small gifts. They give in proportion to their income, which means the gifts are appropriately sacrificial to them. Shadow Christians do this by giving what are commonly called tithes and offerings.

While opinions differ about how to quantify these gifts, those two categories are common to many church-based approaches to giving. A basic percentage—a tithe (10 percent of a person's income)—is foundational giving, usually donated to a church without restrictions or designations. Additional gifts—offerings beyond the tithe—are contributed to special projects, parachurch ministries, schools, camps, and other special needs. Shadow Christians make these gifts willingly and joyfully, knowing God has provided all they have and expects them to channel an appropriate amount to his work.

While wealthy donors and large gifts can be a blessing, the most controversial giving story in the early church involved a prominent person making a public gift. Barnabas, a well-known leader, "sold a field he owned, brought the money, and laid it at the apostles' feet" (Acts 4:37). This still happens today as prominent people sell real estate or convert capital assets to cash and donate them to their church or a ministry organization. What happened next, particularly the result, isn't so common today—thankfully!

Ananias and his wife, Sapphira, also sold a piece of property and donated part of the proceeds to the church. This was a kind and presumably sacrificial gift. But the problem was, in their desire to be spotlight Christians, they lied, telling the church leaders that they hadn't merely donated part of the proceeds but *all* of the proceeds.

Peter confronted Ananias and asked him, "Why has Satan filled your heart to lie to the Holy Spirit and keep back part of the proceeds of the land?" and then concluded, "You have not lied to people but to God" (Acts 5:3–4). The Bible records the sobering aftermath of what happened when a major gift was given for the wrong reasons—like pride, self-promotion, or personal profit. "When he heard these words, Ananias dropped dead" (Acts 5:5) and then "about three hours later, his wife came in, not knowing what had happened" (Acts 5:7). Peter confronted her in a similar way, and she also lied about the sale proceeds and the gift. Then he confronted her by asking, "Why did you agree to test the Spirit of the Lord?" and told her, "'Look, the feet of those who have buried your husband are at the door, and they will carry you out.' Instantly she dropped dead at his feet" (Acts 5:9–10a).

God judges people who lie about their giving. The issue prompting God's judgment wasn't the size of the gift or that it was given publicly. Barnabas wasn't reprimanded for giving a large public gift, thus illustrating it is possible to do this appropriately. Ananias and Sapphira paid with their lives because of their duplicity, not the size of their gift or how it was given.

Shadow Christians are quiet donors who give without fanfare. When temptation to gain attention or control others by your giving rises within you, resist it. You can give large gifts and even be acknowledged for them, but only when your motive is pure, claims related to the value of the gift are substantiated, and furthering God's mission is the goal. Deception can be deadly when vanity eclipses sacrifice.

Your Gifts Matter

These examples from Jesus' life and ministry, along with stories of some of the earliest offerings in church history, underscore the value of gifts from everyday people. It's people like you—schoolteachers, truck drivers, restaurant managers, computer programmers, and pipe fitters— that fund your church and other kingdom enterprises. The foundation for financing global ministry is millions of everyday people who work hard for their money, give generously as their first financial commitment, manage the remainder wisely, and adjust their lifestyle to live as God provides. These shadow Christians believe everything they have comes from God and belongs to him. They are stewards, not owners, and use their resources carefully, since they really belong to God.

Shadow Christians give generously for many reasons but seldom to attract attention to themselves. They give in obedience to God, to meet legitimate needs, and to support projects they believe in. They are loyal and tenacious givers, contributing through good times and bad to the ministries they support. Even when they have given generously, an unusual need will often have them reaching for their wallet to give a little more. After all, when a tornado wipes out a community or an orphaned child needs a meal, shadow Christians find a way to give the money to meet those needs.

Thank you for giving this way! Thank you for disciplined, sacrificial, faithful giving over the years. Thank you for giving through good times and bad both in your life and in your church or the ministries you support. Thank you for being part of the foundation of ministry finance that sustains the global advance of the gospel. Thank you for always finding a way to give a little more to meet a pressing need. Thank you for never wavering on your conviction that God owns it all. Thank you for being a wise steward, making the most of what you have and living frugally so you have something to share with others. Thank you for investing in leaders and sending your best leaders to help others. Thank you for having a kingdom mind-set.

Shadow Christians like you are a conduit for God's resources. They give for the hilarious joy of being part of what God is doing in the world since "God loves a cheerful giver" (2 Cor. 9:7). You know the feeling! When you give, the results fulfill you in meaningful ways. You don't want to spoil it by letting others know too much about your giving. You are content to be part of the silent majority of everyday believers resourcing God's kingdom. Your name may never be on a building, an endowment, or a chapel. The only recognition you may ever get is a contribution statement for tax purposes, which, of course, never includes the extra giving you do by handing cash to a single mother or a college student trying to make ends meet. But that's just fine. As a shadow Christian, you channel God's resources, enjoy doing so, and draw deep satisfaction from the impact your gifts make in the lives of others.

You pay ministry bills, and you are glad God uses you to do it.

Group Discussion

1. What does the phrase "no margin, no ministry" mean to you? Do you agree that thorough financial planning is essential for ministry organizations? Why or why not?

2. How do you feel about talking about money at church or in any ministry context? Why are some people uncomfortable doing this? Share some reasons and discuss them with your group.

3. Do you agree that some ministry leaders overspiritualize financial issues? Have you had a negative experience with this in a church or ministry organization? What did you learn from this experience? Share those insights with your group.

4. Why is it important to facilitate small gifts from many believers? Why does God work this way rather than just through a few wealthy donors? Discuss your ideas with your group.

5. How does the backstory on the Antioch-Jerusalem conflict change your understanding of the nature of the offering given by Antioch? Have you ever given to anyone who opposed you or questioned your legitimacy? Share those stories with your group.

6. What does the phrase "according to their ability" tell you about the offering by the Antioch church members? How is this similar to offerings in your church? Share your perspective with your group.

7. What was the difference between the gifts given by Barnabas and those by Ananias and Sapphira? Why did God judge this couple so harshly? Discuss with your group how this might apply to donors today.

8. As you come to the end of this study, read the final chapter and celebrate being a shadow Christian. Are you content to serve outside the spotlight? What have you learned through this study that changes your perspective on your role in God's kingdom? Pray for the members of your group to apply these insights.

CONCLUSION

CHAPTER 12

STAYING IN THE SHADOWS

*Y*ou matter.

That is the foundational premise for this book. Based on what we have now learned about shadow Christians, let's add an additional clarifying phrase to summarize your role in God's kingdom.

You matter, but making your name well-known doesn't.

Shadow Christians make a significant difference while staying in the shadows. They accomplish more by focusing on fulfilling God's mission than promoting their importance to the mission. They are content to let others stand in the spotlight, doing their part and letting leaders do theirs without undue comparisons, jealousy, or competition undermining relationships and diluting kingdom progress. Shadow Christians stay in their lane, even if it's an out-of-the-way path of anonymous service.

Context Matters

Many of the principles we have discovered about shadow Christians, particularly the attitude motivating their service, are helpful for spotlight leaders as well. In my context, I am a spotlight leader. Writing this book, however, was not about delivering a message from the spotlight to the shadows. My initial study of unnamed characters in the Bible was motivated by a desire to learn to work more effectively outside the spotlight because, in different contexts or settings, spotlight leaders become shadow Christians. My initial goal for this study wasn't writing a book. It was learning how to lead selflessly, without thinking about making my name well-known. Besides this study, my family and recent ministry experiences have also helped shape this perspective in me.

A few years ago, my son Casey went with me to a speaking event. People brought other books I have written and asked me to sign them. They gathered around after my message to ask questions and take pictures. At that event, I was a spotlight Christian on center stage in that context. Later my son said, "Dad, it's been a few years since I was with you at something like this. Man, you're really famous." In the next nanosecond, I felt pride in my accomplishments rising inside me (especially being praised by one of my children!). Then, with his head cocked to one side and a wry smile, Casey added, ". . . among the

Baptists." We laughed heartily, like only a father and son can at an inside joke.

After that night, *famous among the Baptists* became a catchphrase in our family (and has endured for years). When I receive an accolade for public ministry, one of us (including me sometimes!) will remind everyone, "Yep, still famous . . . among the Baptists." When we say this, we are acknowledging the spotlight only shines so far. My niche is, in one sense, large. I am a recognized leader of one of the largest seminaries in the world and in the largest Protestant denomination in the United States. But on the other hand, billions of people have never heard of the Southern Baptist Convention and would not care if they did. So, while the spotlight shines brightly on me in some ways, it's really just a penlight in the global context. *Famous among the Baptists* reminds me not to think too highly of myself, since Baptist public opinion is notoriously fickle. Fame (even a little bit) is fleeting, and no one should embrace it too tightly.

Another ministry experience also reminded me of my relative anonymity. I traveled alone to India, arriving several hours before the rest of the ministry team. While waiting in the airport for them, I realized not one Indian knew or cared who I was, where I was, or why I was there. More than a billion people didn't know my name. Spotlight leaders may be well-known in certain places or among specific people, but in a different context every one of us becomes a shadow Christian. An entire subcontinent failed to notice my arrival—go figure!

All of us, in some way and in some context, are shadow Christians. We can learn the principles and insights in this book and apply them, even as leaders. For shadow Christians, your goal is making an impact when no one knows your name. For spotlight leaders, the goal is leading with a shadow Christian perspective—focusing more on mission accomplishment than personal notoriety. In short, we need to stop trying to make a name for ourselves and focus on making another name famous.

> **All of us, in some way and in some context, are shadow Christians.**

No Other Name

Only one name really matters—Jesus. In the early church the name of Jesus was central to preaching (Acts 2:38; 4:18; 8:12), baptism (Acts 10:48; 19:5), healing (Acts 3:6), and exorcism (Acts 16:18). The church seemed to do everything consequential in the name of Jesus. Paul underscored this when he wrote, "And whatever you do, in word or in deed, do everything in the name of the Lord Jesus, giving thanks to God the Father through him" (Col. 3:17).

The name of Jesus was cited as authority for unity in the church (1 Cor. 1:10), promoting industry and hard work among believers (2 Thess. 3:6), and demonstrating love as a foundational Christian ethic (1 John 3:23). Jesus' name was the source of strength for leaders facing persecution (Acts 21:13) and the content of the message they were forbidden to speak (Acts 4:18). Ultimately, the name of Jesus is the standard by which everyone will be accountable, "For this reason God highly exalted him and gave him the name that is above every name, so that at the name of Jesus every knee will bow—in heaven and on earth and under the earth—and every tongue will confess that Jesus Christ is Lord, to the glory of God the Father" (Phil. 2:9–11).

As a shadow Christian you can make a significant impact when no one knows your name. You do this best when you magnify the only name that matters—Jesus. When you exalt him, you serve his kingdom purposes most effectively. When you speak his name, you access his power to change lives and make an eternal impact.

You matter, but Jesus matters so much more.

Make his name famous!

NOTES

1. While there are some variations in these accounts, many commentators believe this anonymous woman is identified as Mary, the sister of Lazarus, in a similar story (John 12:1–8).

2. Joseph C. Rost, *Leadership for the Twenty-first Century* (Santa Barbara, CA: Praeger, 1993), 102.

These books
and more by
DR. JEFF IORG

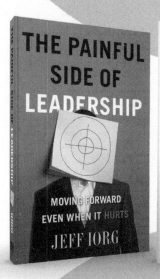

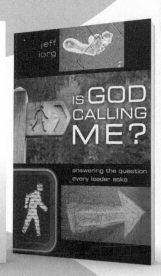